Spiritual counsellor, clairvoyant, h
SPHA healer (Spiritual Pathway Healing Association),
Rebekka Carrolle's warmth and integrity have
transformed many lives with her spiritual gifts and
the powerful influence of the higher realms.

Spiritually aware from an early age Rebekka has faced
many personal challenges, enabling her to help those
who suffer loss, trauma, depression or just need to
find their way back to the right path.

This book will take you through patterns that may
have shaped your life, gently guiding you towards an
enlightened path. No matter where you find yourself
in life, a change of direction is always possible.

Use this book as a tool to embark on a new journey,
discarding fear and negativity. Take time to read
each chapter, digest the content, and then complete
the exercises. Only then can you discard unwanted
emotional baggage.

Learn to embrace and treasure each day, replacing
fear with faith. Become empowered to embrace life's
challenges. Follow Rebekka's philosophy and your life
will never be the same again.

"Blessed be"

Rebekka
23/05/12

Crossing Over
The Bridge

Rebekka Carrolle

A journey from doubt to self-belief

FANTINE PRESS

First published 2010
by
Fantine Press
The Coach House
Stansted Hall
Stansted
Essex CM24 8UD

ISBN 978 1 901958 23 2

Cover illustration by Virginia Whiting

Printed in England by Booksprint

This book is dedicated with heartfelt thanks and infinite gratitude to the memory of two special and gifted men, Gordon Higginson (UK) and John Workman (Barbados).

In my search for the missing "something" within me, I was blessed to meet two very special and gifted men, whose presence left a huge imprint in my life – Gordon Higginson (UK) and John Workman (Barbados). They touched my heart and opened my eyes during their lifetime – and are still continuing to inspire me. They enabled me to cross the bridge of doubt to self-belief, discovering creativity and gifts hidden within the depth of who I am. I have written these pages in my quest to encourage and awaken this potential in others.

My heartfelt thanks also to Brian Timbrell (UK), another gifted man I was destined to meet and who continues to be there for me.

Dear Reader

I have, for as long as I can remember, been like an explorer, searching and seeking, without knowledge of my quarry. I have read books, attended workshops and church services, chatting to many spiritual people of all creeds and cultures in my search for the "missing link."

Life has been good, and sometimes unkind, yet despite heartache, my faith has always been strong. On reflection, there has always been guidance from Above and someone there to reassure and encourage me. Life is for living and seeking the purpose for soldiering on. I am blessed, for I have been privileged to meet and spend precious time with two very special and gifted people whose presence still inspires me, touching my heart and soul.

I realised we find ourselves in situations for a reason. Meetings do not happen by chance; we meet people when it is the right time to meet them. We may prove to be the unknown teacher or perhaps we become the student, sharing laughter, joy, confidences, softening heartache and disappointment. Sometimes we are unaware of the length of time people are meant to share our life.

For the last thirty years, I have quietly been privileged to help people wherever I can, both in UK and abroad. It has been a pathway of discovery, responsibility, joy and delight, whether it is face to face, by post or phone.

At the end of one of my sessions on the Isle of Wight, an older gentleman asked why he was seeing visions of angels. Were they there to help him? This conversation triggered a promise made years ago of sharing my spiritual philosophy – the "missing link" – the joy of finding yourself, and the discovery of serenity and inner peace.

I share with you now elements of a process that will change your thinking and doing, bringing about self-healing in mind, body and spirit, allowing you to cross the bridge of doubt to self-belief.

Relax, enjoy and allow Spirit to uplift you with love and light.

Rebekka

Contents

Introduction

I believe you can come to understand "self" and "others," achieving your highest potential. We live in a time on our planet where varying cultures are vying with each other. Poverty and greed exist side by side; the divide between vast wealth and struggle is apparent in all societies. There appears to be dissention among some religions of the world, so is it any wonder that at times we feel helpless to change the tide? Consequently, it is sometimes very difficult to be the person we truly are or would like to be.

In the age we live in, where the other side of the world is only a jet flight away, it is becoming more and more important to be aware of yourself and others, and to appreciate the wondrous beauty on and around this planet. The complexity and variation in trees, plants, wildlife, sea, sun, moon and stars – all make up this beautiful complex universe we share. Once realisation is awakened, we can reach out and recognise our full potential, finding joy, peace and contentment in being the person we truly are.

Everyone is unique in our looks, thinking, perception of what we visualise and how we perceive the world around us. Identical twins born within seconds of each other still have their own uniqueness, their own free will – we are all individual. That is one of the reasons why living on this planet is so special.

From the time we are born, our senses and visual perception are acute, enabling us to respond to the numerous vibrations around us. We learn very quickly to respond. Without preconceived programming, we recognise the meaning of sounds and their resonance. We respond accordingly to the many elements of love, warmth, food and kindness, safe in the feeling of being nurtured. We unknowingly react to pain, unkindness and cruelty. Nurturing, or lack of, leaves imprints on our early formative years deep in our subconscious.

A toddler taking its first steps may stumble a few times before achieving success. The stumbles do not deter as the need to walk is far greater than the fear of stumbling. Once accomplished, the stumbling is forgotten, success and joy overriding any discomfort or tears. From a very young age we seek encouragement to acquire skills and grow. We learn to emulate those who inspire us, who reassure and spur us on to achieve. The greatest historical figures, irrespective of their background, owe their achievement and inspiration to a situation, guidance from the Higher Realms, a beloved animal or breathtaking scene. Everyone needs an aim, coupled with motivation and determination to achieve. We all need direction and the spark of belief to keep going, especially when the going gets tough.

A lioness will hunt to feed her cubs, often putting her own life at risk as the need to feed the young cubs overrides any unknown danger in the need to nurture the young and stave off starvation. We all have the ability to achieve and to overcome any doubts and fears that for whatever reason prevent us from forging ahead, achieving our full potential, reaching out to our dreams and goals.

Patterning of the past can sometimes result in hesitation and holding back, preventing us from recognising and accepting opportunities when they arise.

I believe this life on earth is a schoolroom; every lesson mastered allows us to move on with confidence and ability to achieve more and more. We need to find courage hidden deep within our being, to recognise and deal with unwelcome patterns, enabling the mind to be free and creative thought to flow. Our innermost thoughts, doubts and fears are unique; no two people share the same thought pattern.

The emotions and inability to express ourselves fully can come from many aspects of our upbringing:

a.   Social standing in community
b.   Family dynamic patterning
c.   Sibling order and rivalry
d.   Desire to fit in and belong
e.   Character personality and interaction

The years seem to fly by, life seeming to move at a faster pace. The pressure on everyone appears to be greater – the need for a new car, a bigger house, an exotic holiday. The tabloids, media and press reinforce the emphasis on spending, creating unspoken pressure on humanity to be part of the throng. Acquisition of "the latest fashion" is subtly driven into our minds by television or cinema, a glance at a newspaper or magazine. The pressure is everywhere! How do you feel acquiring the latest fashion accessory, newly registered car, mixing socially with those considered elite? What were your motives? Were they to demonstrate to the outside world your status, your achievement?

How many times have you taken a journey, reaching your destination on time? Do you recall any impression on the way? Were you observant? Could you describe the journey or were you so focussed on getting from A to B that you were oblivious to the sensations and experiences in between?

Do you realise that by reading these words you are seeking to understand yourself and others? Has it ever occurred to you that this second, this minute, this day is precious and will be lived only once? *You will never again experience this moment*, so it makes sense to welcome, enjoy and make the best of each moment of every day from now on.

The ability to link in with your higher self will enable you to value each day, to look for the good, the positive and unique vibration of each day. Even when life is difficult, there is always a positive vibration if you seek it. Being able to link in with who you are will ensure that you are able to tap into the contentment and peace deep inside and sense a freedom which is magical. *The search reaps wonderful worthwhile rewards.*

The journey of understanding and discovering yourself is uplifting. Allowing your higher self to shine is amazing. The knowledge and wisdom hidden within your depths can blossom and grow. In essence, it is listening to the still, small voice that is crying out to be recognised and heard. You may refer to it as "intuition." What you call it is not important. What is important is that in essence it is "You."

Remember:
"We travel this life only once"
"This day becomes tomorrow's memory"
"Enjoy each day, as the gift of life is life itself"
"The most precious gift you can give anyone and
   which can never be returned is time"

Seek to understand:
Yourself
Other people
Mastering thoughts
– releasing inner peace through self-induced relaxation

Chapter One
Communication With Higher Self

Awareness is knowledge, a communication of trust and peace with your higher self – a perfect blend of who you are. You will all have experienced déjà vu, a vivid dream, a feeling, a knowing, an energy, an awareness that is familiar, learning to accept and trust your higher self is part of an energy force that is indestructible. You are spirit in a physical frame: you are indestructible!

Once you tap into your intuition, over a period of time communication becomes clearer and stronger. Honour and respect your intuition; listen to and act upon the still, small voice within; note its message. You are the essence of spirit, a physical frame, a vehicle of recognition. The power you have within you is real, universal, a God-given power where mind energies live on. You can access this power at any time. Just have faith and believe.

You may have been brought up to believe we are judged when the time comes for us to leave this earth plane and pass to the Higher Realms. I believe we judge ourselves here on earth and later in the Higher Realms. You may choose to ignore or accept the distinction between right or wrong as dictated by your higher self. However, I believe we are responsible for our own actions and accountable for any unkind thought, word or deed.

Can you recall a time where you may have been party to cheating, an untruth, an unkind deed or action? Later, once removed from that situation, reflection harbours awkwardness and often regret – a thought of wishing you could turn back time. I believe it is your conscience, your higher self, reminding you of the universal law that *"whatever we give out is returned to us threefold."* It is fear kicking in, suggesting you acted against your better nature, ignoring your higher self. So from now on be vigilant where your thoughts and actions are concerned. The universal law of karma is real – *"Like attracts like."* Kindness is repaid with kindness, compassion with understanding. You are being reminded to be aware of others, respecting their feelings while considering your own.

A partnership with your higher self heralds deep peace and happiness, and total trust. Your pathway ahead will be true and clear, your higher self guiding you. It is about developing an unquestioning trust. In return, you will be given answers to all problems encountered on a day-to-day basis when the time is right. You will be given all the help and wherewithal to fulfil your needs for your journey ahead.

We are pure energy here to learn lessons. The earth plane is our schoolroom. What may appear on the surface to be decaying is, in fact, recreating energy. All energy moves to a rhythm, a perfect cycle. A forest in winter may appear dead and dormant, with autumn's vegetation lying on the ground. Although supposedly dead, the decaying leaves return nutrients to the soil, providing nourishment to foliage and species inhabiting the forest floor, the forest patiently waiting for the warmth of the spring weather. Nothing is ever wasted. Everything happens as it is ordained to do so; everything happens at the right time. Wouldn't it be bizarre if daffodils decided to bloom in the height of summer! Everything on this plane is connected to the God source – everything vibrates at the right frequency.

You all have this wonderful energy. Learn to tap into it. Allow it to be part of you. Welcome its presence, nurturing dormant gifts and talents, waiting to be used for your future enrichment. Once you link into this awareness, this wonderment, problems will seem minuscule; you will be rich beyond belief, facing problems and challenges with faith and acceptance.

Learn to:

- Blend energies
- Trust energies
- Balance emotional self
- Communicate clearly with yourself and others
- Have clarity in decision-making

Life's journey can sometimes be bumpy. When these times arise, note a change in your energies. Disappointments, sadness, bereavement, upset and tiredness will affect the energy of this wonderful newly found power. So learn to be aware of your own needs and "to listen."

If you are in physical pain, frustrated, angry or unhappy, ask yourself:

- What is the cause?
- Could it be lifestyle, diet or environment?
- An inability to verbalise true feelings?

The essence of this wonderful discovered power, wisdom and knowledge is that it is with you all the time:

- Trust it and tap into it – it is unique to you
- This power is universal energy and indestructible
  Blockages and problems are created by doubt and lack of trust

There is negative and positive in all things. You will learn to sense, to understand spiritual law where "negative attracts negative and positive attracts positive." You may recall that if you spend time with a pessimist, before long your thoughts too take on a negative slant. By the same token, you will feel uplifted when spending time with an optimist. Unknowingly, your thoughts and ideas will expand.

Feel the expansion of consciousness; look for the best in every situation. Personalities differ; people on a spiritual pathway see every day as a new experience, every frustration and obstacle a challenge to be met. One needs to put aside the analytical mind to surrender to who you are. A frog is a frog; it jumps into the pond and acts like frogs do. Human beings need to be "being" rather than "doing" all the time.

Discover your purpose; find balance in your life. The cycle of life can be likened to the seasons. Listen to your body clock, stop when you need to rest and listen to your needs of the day. Trust the power of love through vision and trust.

- Learn to love yourself so others are drawn to your love
- Treasure and cherish yourself
- Accept yourself as yourself
- Be open and accepting of who you are

By allowing another level of awareness to manifest itself, change will come about. The psychological state of self is vast – explore it with relish. You owe it to yourself to live this life to the full, enjoying every moment. Allowing the spiritual part of you to take over enhances inner peace and happiness. You are unique, a precious link in the chain of life so give thanks for the miracle you are.

**REMEMBER THAT GOD IS WITHIN
EVERYONE AND EVERYTHING**

Love

Love is a strength, silent and bold
Unswerving, bright, like pieces of gold
Strong to set pulses racing at a rate
To cherish, to care, to give and to wait

To love is to give all of yourself
Without stopping to count the cost to oneself
To want to be with, to touch and share
Those precious moments so fleeting and dear

Love the emotion, pride at a birth
Tears of joy, happiness, thanks to the earth
For perfection and trust of a new life
Warmth and serenity, no awareness of strife

Love is caring for a special brood
Guarding, guiding, teaching them to be good
Supporting, giving upliftment when needs must
Safe in the knowledge of love and trust

Falling in love is just like pure gold
A precious unity forever to hold
To plan, to share, to always treasure
Life's ups and downs given in measure

Without the circle of love on this earth
It is a long, lonely life from moment of birth
We need to be loved, to be told that one cares
A smile, a hug, a kiss unawares

So love your family, friends as well
Tell them you care, giving hugs as well
Your reward a rich, warm glow deep inside
For love of God and man is difficult to hide.

Chapter 2
Awakening the Senses

Awareness is discovering your higher self, a blending of your conscious and unconscious mind. It will take time; the journey will be challenging, exciting and uplifting. It is not about being egotistical, dominant or powerful. It is about you being aware of who you are, recognising your potential and being in touch with inspiration, becoming aware of the energy you transmit to the world, and in turn becoming aware of others around you and the energy they transmit.

Everyone is psychic no matter what creed, culture or social status. Some are aware at an early age, some never listen, and in some the awareness lies dormant waiting to be awakened at the right time. The joy of awareness is for you to experience, to enjoy the powerful force that is within you.

Are you truly aware of your senses?

To hear	–	*musical notes, pitch of voices, birdsong, baby crying, people laughing, jet engine, sea breaking on the shore*
To see	–	*beauty of Mother Earth, antics of pets, birds in flight, facial expressions*
To feel	–	*joy, happiness, sadness, pain, disappointment, rejection, fear, elation*
To smell	–	*fresh baked bread, flower fragrance, freshly mown grass, pine cones, sea ozone, freshly laundered sheets*
To touch	–	*salty wetness of the sea, rough sandpaper, softness of newborn skin, dry sand, fabric, paper, fur, plants, soil, pebbles*
To taste	–	*sweet honey, juicy fruits, salty anchovies, hot chilli peppers, spicy curry, sharp lemon juice*
To sense	–	*inner emotions, mood of others, imprint of buildings, presence of angels, presence of spirit guides, love, closeness of passed relatives, pets' love and devotion.*

Mankind has evolved through aeons of time. We are now experiencing vast change, a period of materialism with more changes on the horizon. Mother Nature has unleashed her power many times in the past, changing this planet beyond recognition and will at some time give us a repeat performance. We benefit from the explosion of brilliant entrepreneurs and the technological ideas we use yet we are reminded, from time to time, out of the blue, that God and Mother Nature are firmly in control and mankind is helpless to intervene.

The Perceived Upside – Multicultural integration, the ability to acquire more and more, increased technology – powerful cars, faster communication, the ability to reach destinations quickly. We take for granted time-saving contraptions, copious gallons of clean water, hot water at the turn of a tap, central heating warmth, leisure parks, jet flight, clean clothes, furnishings, hair and beauty products, and the availability of fruit and vegetables from around the world. Supermarkets and shopping malls are open day and night, offering tempting quick, easy meals. They display a variety of merchandise to reinforce that we "must have" the many products on offer – in essence to encourage us to spend, spend, spend!

The Real Downside – Sadly, we have lost sight of the damage mankind is doing to Mother Earth. Many animals are now extinct due to climate change and the indiscriminate disappearance of their habitat, illustrating once again mankind's lack of care, selfishness and greed. The rain forests, jungles and their wildlife are trampled on and destroyed in the never-ending quest for more and more. Regretfully, the carefree, simplistic lifestyle of many recently discovered hidden tribes, completely oblivious to modern civilisation, is now tainted and destroyed. Responsibility rests with twenty-first century man and this modern materialistic, technological age we have become part of.

Pause for Thought – Is today's world really making mankind happy, offering peace and contentment, with joy and desire to welcome each new day? Are we now questioning historical actions? Could that be why many of us are searching and seeking an unknown "something"? Many people are now reasoning, *"Is this really what life is all about?"* Could that be the reason why many are flocking back to "the simple life" where they find joy in preparing a meal from homegrown produce? Remembering the freshness, taste, variety and sense of achievement in growing fruit and vegetables in a recently created vegetable plot. Revisiting a memory of spending time with relatives in the country, stirring memories of a different lifestyle, family unity, hard at times, but rewarding ones.

Could that be why many high achievers are disillusioned, where the acquisition of big money no longer holds the attraction it once did, feeling the need to turn their back on the fast pace, choosing to rethink and relocate to a more relaxed lifestyle in the countryside? Trying to discover time for each other, searching for the inner peace and contentment they now acknowledge is missing from their lives.

A balance needs to be found. We are grateful for modern advances and many of us would now find life odd and difficult without all the trappings now available. Sad to say, many are inwardly dissatisfied and unhappy, the realisation dawning of the need to find the missing link, of finding "the inner self," which is vital in regaining the balance sorely missing in many people's lives. In essence, they are searching to be in touch with their inner spiritual self, their senses.

When was the last time you took the opportunity to be STILL?
To hear the SILENCE?
To sense the SILENCE?
To knowingly discover that the sound of SILENCE is pure magic?
Take time out to LISTEN AND BE AMAZED!

How many of you really see what is around you? Do you really drink in what you are seeing – whether it is a woodland setting, strolling by the seashore or simply gazing at the magnificent coloured sky as the sun goes down? Appreciate and really see the home you have created. Delight in the order and brilliance of life and colour in your garden, repaying your hard endeavours. Acknowledge and appreciate the warmth and companionship of friends, pets and family.

NOW STOP READING. CLOSE YOUR EYES AND LISTEN.

WHAT DO YOU HEAR AND SENSE?

HEAR   –   Outside noise – the gentle rhythm of your breath, your heartbeat.

TOUCH   –   Your skin – is it warm, clammy, hot or cold?

FEEL   –   Silence, inner peace, flow of your breath safe, love, upliftment, peace.

SEE   –   Visual images, colour, visualisation

Exercise – Sensing
(Write down your thoughts and feelings)

The sounds you hear at night before you fall asleep:

\- -

\- -

\- -

\- -

\- -

\- -

\- -

\- -

\- -

\- -

\- -

\- -

\- -

\- -

\- -

The sounds outside your home at the end of the day:

_ _

_ _

_ _

_ _

_ _

_ _

_ _

_ _

_ _

_ _

_ _

_ _

_ _

_ _

_ _

_ _

_ _

_ _

Waking in the morning, what sounds do you hear? How do you feel?

Listen

Do you really listen to what people say
Or are your thoughts far away?
Do you really care for someone else
Or are you thinking of yourself?

It's amazing what one can learn
Being silent and still one can earn
The friendship and trust of another being
As they open their heart to their inner feelings

Being a good listener needs lots of skill
To care enough to watch, keeping very still
Giving confidence and reassurance
To the talker so full of effervescence

All people need is a good listening ear
To know someone really cares
A problem shared is a problem halved
No faltering, no holds barred.

So be a friendly soul when you can
Give warmth to a child or the elderly man
For everyone needs to be needed and know
The listener cares enough to let it show

So put yourself in another's shoes
Learn people both love and lose
So remember every moment you impart
Is a little of you given from the heart

Chapter 3
Recharging Your Energies

Energy is life

All life is vibration and energy. Every living organism follows a natural rhythmic cycle of birth and rebirth. We are all part of a whole. Mother Earth is the third planet from the sun and the only planet known to us on which life is known to exist and yet is only one of thousands of planets and stars in the universe. New planets and stars are formed; old ones die to come into existence again in a different form. I believe we all chose to live this life on our truly remarkable, magnificent and wondrous planet.

All life moves in cycles, being part of the natural law of regeneration, energies being replenished, new growth taking place, where we are physically renewed or reborn. Your body also goes through stages of growth – babyhood, childhood, adolescence and adult. It is believed there are seven ages of man and a seven-year cycle of regeneration. These phases may come and go without trials and tribulation yet it is important during these phases to explore the past and deal with matters of the present while reaching out to the future. During these cycles, we need to recognise and deal with issues we acknowledge as being inhibiting, clearing the way for the journey ahead (*Chapter 12 – Clearing the Path*).

Our birth certificate gives date of birth, place of birth and parentage. When we are young, it is a natural progression to mark birthdays or a milestone with a celebratory flourish, especially at the ages of eighteen and twenty-one. But as we go through our life, the milestones can appear to be a mountain range. They are approached with fear rather than acceptance, with grace, wisdom and the wealth of experience gained on the journey of life so far. Clear perception and attitude to challenges is the key to a happy, contented and successful life.

Recently, I met a lady who fervently believed that when she reached the age of sixty, she was old. She recalled her mother became old at that age, acting and dressing her age. She perceived herself to be in the same frame. Her approach to life changed, her zest for living, her desire for learning something new. Her belief was so strong in her mind that the future of a bright tomorrow had disappeared. She recalls being enthralled by adventure stories and fairy tales, mesmerised by watching the film the "Wizard of Oz." However, the pattern of being old at the age of sixty was so ingrained in her subconscious that she acted accordingly. Sad to say, she felt she was too old to change the patterning of a lifetime and was not receptive to change. Life is for living. Using age as a barrier to enjoying life's journey exists only in the mind.

The expected span of living has changed. The accepted longevity being three score and ten is now outmoded. Some say the age of seventy is considered young. It is now accepted to consider people being elderly at eighty-plus. This shift is partly due to technology, a change in people's perception and circumstance, and opportunities to seek, discover and partake of interests and journeys which would, in the past, have seemed impossible. Jet travel, the internet and media coverage have expanded horizons, creating travelling opportunities to explore cultures and fulfil dreams. They are available to those who have the desire and wherewithal to take advantage of this new found freedom.

Balancing energies in mind, body and spirit is vital. This is easily done by being honest with yourself, looking at your lifestyle, addressing matters and issues needing attention, weighing up the pros and cons of a situation, and removing restrictions that prevent you from achieving your goal of being happy and content. We all go through phases in life where we tend to shoulder too much responsibility, accommodating other people's wishes to the detriment of our own. How often have you agreed to do something, only to later regret and perhaps resent the deed you willingly agreed to take on? This process does require raw honesty and courage, but is a valuable lesson in becoming the person you truly are. Mastering the use of the word "No!" is difficult, especially to people you care for and respect, but is worth the effort. You will be in control, finding that people respect you and your word, the pressure on your lifestyle easing. It will be a learning curve for all involved.

Being a muse and mentor to others is an art. Encouraging others to take responsibility for their own decisions and actions is sometimes awkward and difficult, especially when loved ones are involved, but essential for all concerned. Success means achieving balance. Mastering life and its complexities is like making a huge fruit cake. Some people take time, carefully sourcing the best quality ingredients whilst others are happy to improvise, making do with items in the store cupboard and a few purchased from a local shop. Some use scales to weigh the exact measure of ingredients whilst others guess the amount. The recipe may be the same, but the end result is very different. Each is edible, one perhaps lighter and moist in texture, both being rich, but tasting very different. What is important is looking carefully at your life, accepting responsibilities, prioritising and acknowledging matters you find irksome. Look within – make necessary adjustments and changes to benefit YOU, a very important and precious soul.

Changes inevitably take place during the many cycles of our life. There are periods when we are full of energy, upbeat, light-hearted, still, lonely, despondent or isolated. Listen to your body's natural rhythm; go with the flow of energies. If you are tired, stop! Recognise and take advantage of bursts of inspirational energy. The body of every human being is unique in size, complexion, characteristics and colouring. Our energies respond to different stimuli and need to be balanced. We care for our high performance cars, book a regular service and MOT, and replace worn out parts, ensuring optimum performance. Do we take the same care of our body? Although beings of light, our body is how people recognise us. The vehicle of recognition we were born with is seen by others and us every day. It makes sense to love and care for it. In essence, to find balance.

Tired energies need to be recharged. To create the perfect balance, you need to listen to your body, your cycle and rhythm. Some people are "larks" – they wake up with the lark and are best in the morning. Others are like "owls" and function best later on in the day and at night. Some are neither one nor the other and achieve energy balance all through the day. To determine your own needs, creating balance, you need to listen to your own body cycle and rhythm.

Irrespective of culture or creed, essentially our needs are the same:

- *Food – Essential in providing mental nourishment or stimulus, vital for our very existence.*

We need to nurture the body that is so valuable to us, maintaining fitness and optimum energy. Some foods more than others are tolerated and accepted by our digestive system. Most foods we enjoy eating make us feel great, but some tend to cause discomfort and are best either eliminated from your diet or taken in moderation. Certain groups of foods can cause a strong allergic reaction and need to be avoided. Listen to your body; it will dictate the foods easily assimilated and those suspect foods your body finds difficulty in tolerating. Diet gurus are constantly telling us not to eat this or that, but listen to your own body. Enjoy the foods that make you feel good and are easily digested. Listen to your bodily needs, accepting how different foods affect you.

Alcohol is a stimulant and relaxant, and sometimes a confidence booster, allowing inhibitions to diminish. In small doses, it is a tonic. In excess, it can cause problems so be sensible and limit your intake.

• **Sleep** – *A state of quiescence or dormancy, a periodic state of physiological rest during which consciousness is suspended.*

When young, we have all pushed the boundaries of our existence, burning the candle at both ends, resulting in very little sleep. A good night's sleep is vital in recharging our battery. Restless sleep is disruptive, as is having a lot on our mind. Consequently, mental concentration and general countenance suffer. A good sleeping pattern is beneficial. The experts state that the average person benefits from seven hours' sleep at night. Listen to your body, as it is your best barometer. It is well known that some people can exist quite happily on only a few hours of sleep at night. This may be due to family genes or a sleeping pattern created from childhood. Comparing your sleep pattern with those of your parents and siblings can usually provide the answer. Listen to your natural body clock.

• **Socialising** – *Friendly, companionable opportunity for friendship and conviviality.*

A social life is vital for general well-being. Interaction with others is an opportunity to express yourself, to laugh, exchange views, trigger new interests and spark a wave of enthusiasm. Without friends, it is easy to become insular. If you are shy, be gentle with yourself. Mix with people you feel comfortable with. Once confidence is gained, you can gradually integrate into a wider social circle.

- ***Hobbies*** – *Activities pursued in spare time for pleasure or relaxation.*

It is beneficial to have an interest, a pursuit, an opportunity to try something new, to spend some quiet time away from home and work. Absorption in a pastime or recreation where purpose and pleasure is achieved brings much enjoyment and contentment. People who tend not to pursue an activity, hobby or outside interest find the weeks quite dull, with time appearing to stand still. They suffer from a lack of stimulus and social interaction, and a restricted network of friends.

- ***Harmony in the work environment*** – *Doing or making something – a job, trade or task undertaken, paid employment.*

We live in a material world, the medium of exchange functioning as legal tender being money as against trading a trade as in days gone by. We need to have a monetary income to pay for food, home, clothes, warmth, education, clean water and social pleasure. Unfortunately, there are large groups of people who work hard, performing a job of work they would rather not do, but forced to stay for the pay packet at the end of the week. There are, however, those who choose a career they enjoy and feel passionate about. They spend their working lifetime following a career path they really enjoy. Even in a work situation, it is advantageous to balance material reality with harmony where possible.

It is a well known fact that on balance people spend a larger proportion of their time at work than at home, so the importance of achieving harmony at work is paramount. The complete working package impacts on your life – the location, ambience of the environment, working colleagues, travelling distance from home to work, opportunity for career progression, job benefits and prospects. All these factors combine to impress upon your mind how you view your job of work. Ideally, you need to seek a package of balance suited to your individual personality and needs.

Feng shui is the Chinese art of determining propitious design and placement of a building or room so that maximum harmony is achieved between the flow of the ch'i (animating living energy, constantly moving through the cycles of life) of the environment, benefiting the user. This ancient art is believed by many to promote prosperity and optimism. The key changes recommended by experts for large organisations result in increased productivity, benefiting employer and employees alike.

- **Harmony in the home** *– A place where one can be at ease: living in a family group.*

There are very few of us who are fortunate enough to be living in their dream home. Be thankful for your home. It is somewhere you lay down your head at night and a reflection of you and your family. Your attitude to life impacts on family members sharing your home. If you are calm and content, everyone else will instinctively follow suit. Energy is transferable. If you are dissatisfied with a particular matter, need to make a decision or ideally would like to make changes, then be positive, seek some valuable quiet time, cogitate and allow new thought patterns to emerge to enable changes to manifest. If studying is laborious, focus on the end result; strive to achieve your dream.

- **Pets** *– A tame animal or creature kept for companionship and amusement.*

Cherished, affectionate, unconditional love – words to describe a much-loved creature. Pets become an important part of the family. Enjoy their presence; cherish their existence; enjoy and delight in the unconditional love they so willingly give. Be aware of the enormous impact they have on your life.

When we lose them through accident, illness or old age, we are devastated. We grieve for the loss of the loyality, companionship and unconditional love they graciously gave. So enjoy and relish their love. An animal is often the sole companion to a person living on his or her own. Sadly, the only interaction a person may have is to share thoughts and feelings with their beloved pet, enjoying the reciprocal daily interaction vital to their survival, inner peace and life itself.

I lost my beloved Siamese cat, Saatchi, a week after moving house. I sobbed for weeks and still become emotional when memories cloud my mind. I miss him greeting me when he heard my key in my front door. I relive his distinctive voice, mannerisms, character, love and companionship. I am truly blessed for we enjoyed nearly nineteen years together – a testament to his devotion to me. I know his essence is always close by and hear him from time to time, but still miss his presence. What is important when we lose irreplaceable pets is to treasure the good times and the happy memories.

- ***Time*** – *Mankind's word for the continuous passage of existence in which events pass from the finality of the past to the state of now, the present, to the potentiality of the future.*

We live our lives by the clock – a measure of time and to some a curse of the modern world. When we look back at the passage of human existence, time seems to be gone in the wink of an eye. The hands of a clock constantly remind us that another second, another minute has gone by. They are a continual register of time.

The impact and significance of time is different to everyone and their situation. Awaiting the birth of a baby is nerve-wracking, with time slowing down. Time drags when waiting at a bus stop in the rain when the bus is late.

When taking an important examination, time gallops. For the frail in a hospital bed, time drags, the passage of time only broken by a smile and cup of tea. Waiting for that important telephone call, time appears to stand still. Whatever time means to you, in whatever circumstances you find yourself, be aware time is so very precious; it can never be recovered, so grasp it with both hands.

- ***Me*** – *Personality and expression of the speaker or writer.*

Everyone, irrespective of age, speaks of life speeding up. Living in this century is exciting, challenging and sometimes exhausting, reinforcing the need for "Me" time, precious quality time to allow your thoughts and feelings to flow.

Loving, being loved and knowing someone so well is truly wonderful. It somehow reinforces the justification for allocating some quality time for you, allowing space and time to be alone with your own thoughts, building the link with your higher self. You can cogitate during this special time, resolving concerns or worries you may have. It is valuable time spent assimilating thoughts and feelings, regenerating your energy, your vitality, sensing inner peace. Time for yourself is vital, giving yourself permission to be in touch with the very essence of who you are. You are not being selfish; you owe it to yourself to set aside some quality "Me" time.

- **_Reserve_** – _To keep back or set aside for future contingencies._

The weight of responsibilities thrust upon us at work, home, family and loved ones unwittingly make huge demands on our time and energy. These unforeseen demands often come from unexpected sources: illness, redundancy, emergency medical care, financial worries or family commitments all necessitate the need for us to tap into our reserve contingency of energy.

Most motorists today have the sense to ensure their petrol or diesel tank is relatively full most of the time in the eventuality there is a need to drive somewhere quickly. By listening to your body clock, allowing time for yourself and maintaining a positive attitude to life, you will always have some energy in reserve for emergencies. Stored reserved energy will then always be available for you to tap into it when the need arises, enabling you to meet unexpected and unforeseen situations with calm and confidence.

We all have short bursts of insight and intuition. By being aware of the inner you, your awareness will be heightened. You will learn to listen and trust your inner voice on a day-to-day basis, allowing the insight to guide and reassure you with everyday life's challenges. This will subtly create an inner state of peace and contentment with an eventual knowing of a wisdom and knowledge deep within acknowledging that what you feel is "real."

Remember:

We are not physical beings having a spiritual experience

We are spiritual beings having an earth experience

Exercise – Recharging your energies:
When is your energy flow at its best?

— —

— —

— —

— —

— —

— —

— —

— —

— —

— —

— —

— —

— —

— —

— —

When is your energy flow at its lowest?

How do situations affect your energy flow?

Time

Time is a measure, time is a measure
Time is a measure of pleasure to treasure
Like the ticking of the old school clock
And the court clock in the magistrates' dock

Time for the frail is a long, long day
Waiting for meals provided each day
A smile, a few words the day's highlight
Before pill-popping time to secure a good night

Time for the commuter is one fast pace
Rushing to the city, a place in the rat race
Computers, fax machines, telephones lines
Plush fancy offices, part of the shrine

Busy mums getting their brood off to school
Uniform, lunch box, don't forget the rule
Settling down to the housework routine
Boring necessity before lunch of baked beans

The struggling business with the galloping clock
The shepherd busy tending his flock
Paperboy, postman, milkman too
All rushing to deliver their wares to you

The motorway pace is by far the best
Three lanes full, no one wants to be last
Motorists impatient, honking their horns
Ambulance siren, a baby to be born

Everyone, everywhere, gets tired of the push
Ends the day weary, seeking plenty of hush
Time to unwind before going to bed
Best part of the day as you lay down your head.

Drat that clock, it's gone off again
Bother the dark, the sound of the rain
Rushing again to fight off the fray
Time is only a measure of a new day

Chapter 4
Harmonising Body & Breath

Breathing, an involuntary act, is a vital function we do every minute of every day. Without it we could not survive. We can live without food for weeks and survive without water and sleep for days, but how long can we live without breathing?

Our breath is vital to the function of the human body and the means through which we can access higher awareness. The deeper and slower our breathing, the easier it becomes to work at higher levels of awareness, increasing an ability to access deep knowledge and understanding.

Where possible, it is best to breathe in air through the nose rather than the mouth, as the nose is designed to filter any impurities in the air. This filter also warms and moistens the air as it travels towards the lungs. To illustrate this point, if you breathe through your mouth on a cold winter's day, you will be aware of the effort of breathing, especially if you take a sharp intake of breath while undertaking a strenuous task. Generally, unless we are taught and trained, we only use part of our lung capacity.

Trained singers are given exercises to help them use their full lung capacity and control their breathing during a performance. As you exhale, the diaphragm (the muscle partition that separates the abdominal and thoracic cavities) curves inwards and upwards, helping to force the unwanted air out of the lungs. Unfortunately, this muscle is the least used. Learning to breathe correctly is very important in assisting your awareness and psyche development.

Remember all exercises need to start gradually. It is very important to be mindful of this, especially if you are trying a new breathing rhythm for the first time. In the event you feel slightly dizzy or a little light-headed, wait for five or ten minutes and allow your body time to readjust. Then try again. Be gentle with yourself at this time. Patiently build a new changing breathing rhythm slowly.

Relax – Put all your worries and concerns into an imaginary box outside the door. They are safe for you to collect later, should you so wish.

1. *Close your eyes and relax your body. Starting with your shoulders, slowly visualise linking with the energy and purpose of each group of muscles, major organs and limbs of your body until you reach your feet. Consciously focus on the wonderful miracle of how your limbs, vital interconnecting muscles and major organs work together to maintain a balanced healthy body. Now focus on your breath.*

2. *Focus on a rhythm of gentle, comfortable breaths, gradually increasing in depth. As each breath deepens, visualise each breath oxygenating deep within your very being. Now imagine filling every muscle, organ and limb in your body with pure white light where all impurities, negatives, discomfort and pain are filtered and removed.*

3. *You should now feel relaxed, conscious of your breathing settling into a comfortable, gentle rhythm. With your eyes closed, place your hands on your solar plexus, the part of the stomach beneath the diaphragm (known as pit of the stomach), fingertips lightly touching. Relax. Be conscious of your breathing. Slowly and gently, also be aware of the inner calm enveloping you. Imagine you are breathing in pure white light. Visualise this soft healing light surrounding you. Sense the warmth, peace, tranquillity, its enveloping power and intensity. You are safe.*

Exhale softly, silently repeating this image in your mind every time you take a breath. Gently visualise this wonderful light encapsulating every part of your body until you are completely enclosed in a bubble of pure white light. Feel the light dissipate pain, concerns, cares and discomfort.

RELAX AND ENJOY

Be comfortable. Be still. Enjoy the moment. Be conscious of the lightness of your physical frame, the wonderful sense of peace and calm. Be conscious of your breathing rhythm. Be centred and still.

Once mastered, this simple exercise awakens and heightens the senses.
> *For every intake of breath, count to four (five)*
> *Hold the breath for a count of four (five)*
> *Exhale for a count of four (five)*
> *Repeat*

Mastering this exercise requires practice. Be gentle and patient with yourself, especially if this is a new experience and you are consciously focussing on the breath for the first time. Commence with a count of three, gradually building up to a count of five.

Be conscious of the inner peace and calm flowing through your body. Mastering this breathing exercise, you will soon notice a significant change in your well-being and how you think and feel in attuning the mind, body and spirit.

Be conscious of the breath, an essential life force oxygenating your body.

> Our body is the temple of God
> Our mind the altar of God
> Our spirit an embodiment of God

Be conscious of your unique power to love and cherish who you are.

Take the first step in changing your life by being aware of your breath. By consciously focussing your mind onto your breathing, subtle, positive changes will take place in your thinking and doing. By attentively falling into a new deep breathing rhythm, your life will gradually change without you giving it a conscious thought.

Mastering a new breathing pattern allows another level of awareness to become manifest. The psychological state of self is so vast. The West is only now beginning to catch up with the teachings of mystics and seers of the East, who have used these and other techniques for centuries, enabling followers to reach a deep awareness in their quest to understand themselves, the universe and all metaphysics.

In the past, people were content for a spiritual gift to become manifest. Great seers and mystics were respected and allowed to use their insight. You, too, will come to realise the profound impact this simple exercise will have on your life in strengthening your intuition, increasing clarity in decision-making.

YOU ARE UNIQUE – YOU ARE IMPORTANT

You owe it to "**YOU**" to allow yourself time to gain understanding and be yourself

Learning to be still and aware of your unique powerful energy while focussing on your breathing – especially during a time of peaceful meditation – leads to a wonderful sense of peace and contentment. Matters of a psychological nature causing concern will gradually be put in perspective and answers eventually found.

There are many instances when becoming conscious of your breathing helps on a day-to-day basis. You may have been told in the past to *"Count to ten before you speak."* This saying came about purely to allow a brief span of time to reason thoughts and feelings before replying. This is especially beneficial when an important question is fired at you, the answer being of vital consequence. When you find yourself under stress and pressure, remember to focus on your breathing just for a few moments to allow your body and mind to be still, and thoughts and feelings assessed, before responding. Eventually, the awareness and benefits of your new breathing rhythm will become second nature.

The teachings and doctrines of the Eastern mystics have always influenced its people's thinking and doing. Its relevance is still respected and adhered to in today's materialistic 21st century. Many in the Western world anxiously seek to understand their teaching, respect and beliefs, the desire to understand seemingly even more prevalent in this fast technological age.

Expectations of ourselves and other people's expectations of us are increasing, so in this fast-fuelled pace of life, it is becoming more and more crucial to find a way of coping with the stress and pressure alongside fulfilling our purpose while discovering who we are.

The way we lead our life is important and as significant as discovering who we are. What makes us "tick"? How many of you try to be the person everyone wants you to be, the still, small voice inside you screaming "Help!"

Awareness enhances the spiritual part of you – the very essence of who you are. Once realisation dawns, doubts and confusion disappear, clarity reigns regarding choices and decisions, the pathway ahead becoming clear and attainable. You need to love the essence of who you are to use and recognise talents bestowed upon you – to be your own person, for everyone's good, enabling you to be a key player, empowering you to make a mark on this wonderful world. By the same token, you need to understand and recognise the qualities and talents in others. This recognition is infinite. The source is infinite, leading us from untruth to truth.

a. You are unique. Be in touch with your higher self.
b. Changing your life and being **YOU** is so important.
   Be the miracle you are.
c. All life interconnects as we pass through it.
   Boundaries are merely "physical."
   Doubts and fears in the mind hinder our progress.
d. Remember that we are naturally drawn to people who blend and harmonise with our energies
   People feel comfortable associating with like-minded people.

During our life's journey, we meet and share passages of time with many, many people from all walks of life. Some people we meet always remain part of our life; some stay alongside for a short time; some for longer. Have you ever wondered why? I truly believe that everything happens for a reason, coincidence and synchronicity walking hand in hand.

"We meet someone for a reason, a brief period or a lifetime"

Discovering who you are is exciting and a little bit scary, especially if you feel out of step with your family and friends. Be reassured for I believe that each and every one has their very own angel, a guardian angel always there just for you. Your impression of this angel is privy only to yourself. I believe this guardian angel agreed to be close by prior to your moment of birth and is never far away, offering reassurance, guidance and support when needed and called upon, and with you to the end of your lifespan on earth. We need to trust their wisdom, light and energy, especially when difficult decisions and choices are on the horizon. The acknowledgment, closeness and trust achieved during your lifetime is entirely up to you.

Regular meditation brings about a wonderful sense of serene contentment – an inner peace. You will sense colours and visualise beautiful places. You will also discover peaceful knowing, a belonging. You may sense the loving presence of someone close to you. Just accept. Leave your mind open. *Trust.*

Exercise – Breath & Body
Note changes in breathing rhythm after practising new breathing rhythm for
seven days

Note any changes in sleeping pattern

Note changes in your perception of life

_ _

_ _

_ _

_ _

_ _

_ _

_ _

_ _

_ _

_ _

_ _

_ _

_ _

_ _

_ _

_ _

_ _

_ _

Guidance

Do not be afraid for I am here
Waiting to show you a pathway so clear
So bright, so straight, so full of love
Encircled by loved ones, enriched with love

We know exactly where you are
How you feel, sending energy from afar
Greeting you with outstretched arms,
Guiding you away from earthly harm

To enter a new world full of light
A light so brilliant and oh, so bright
Revealing coloured effervescence of every hue
A special designated moment especially for you.

Don't shed a tear for God is near
Do not feel sad, have no fear
Loved ones and guides are waiting to sing
As you trust the care of an angel's wing

A nicer person one couldn't wish to meet
You give love and laughter to all you greet
The legacy of love you leave behind
Being a wondrous gift difficult to find.

So awaken soon to a new rebirth
Blessings from heaven, far from the earth
The celestial realms soon to rejoice with glee
The moment your spirit is truly free

Chapter 5
Invisible Journey

You will now be aware of the importance of being YOU. This awareness and knowledge will be enhanced through meditation. By meditating regularly, you will lower your blood pressure, feel calmer and be aware of what is really happening around you. Your awareness will be heightened. In essence, you will be contacting your stillness within.

Find a time when it is right for you and your family. Find a peaceful environment with no telephones. Let the family know it is your time – a **Me Time** – and ask them to respect your time.

Devote your attention to your point of focus. You can start with, say, five minutes, increasing the time sitting to suit yourself. If you decide to sit for ten minutes, tell yourself just that. You will be amazed at how accurate the time sitting will be. Once confident, you can adjust the time you decide to sit to suit yourself. Sitting on a regular basis is most beneficial.

Do not force your mind to concentrate. Relax. Remember to put all your concerns, worries and pressures of the day in an imaginary box outside the door. You can collect them later.

Music feeds the soul, so they say. The varying moods of music certainly stir the emotions, so if you choose to meditate to music, find a piece you enjoy.

Mystics believe meditation is the path to self-enlightenment. Deep meditation gives you the power to calm the busy mind and be in touch with the inner you. It enables you to concentrate your thoughts rather than chasing them around and around. This level of clarity is essential for self-mastery – it is a magical freedom.

a) Choose a relaxing environment
b) Choose a comfortable position in a chair or on the floor
c) Wear comfortable clothing, loose around the waist to allow energy to flow
d) Wear socks or be bare-foot
e) Create a peaceful ambience – soft lighting, closed curtains
f) Candlelight is a gentle light, soothing and relaxing, and sets the mood
g) Place both feet firmly on the floor. Do not cross your feet or legs as this restricts the energy flow
h) Adjust cushions. Place hands gently in front of you with palms up or down, whichever feels most comfortable

BE AT EASE   RELAX
CLOSE YOUR EYES
CONCENTRATE ON YOUR BREATHING

Meditation, the art of reflection and contemplation of spiritual matters, brings about a wonderful sense of peace, a remarkable induced peace. Practised regularly, this contemplation draws light towards you. You can journey to wherever you choose to go. The impressions stay with you. It is now scientifically proven to be beneficial in aiding healing, changing your mindset and your life.

By utilising your power, you can seek clarity. Believe in your power. Each meditation is different, personal to the individual, the image and impression experienced being invisible to others. Even in a group setting where you share the moment and sensation of being at peace, the experience is unique to each individual. Eventually, you will embark on an opening interlude that feels right for you, one that empowers you to move deeper and deeper into your chosen meditation.

You can, if you so wish, record the following visualisation to meditate to at a later date, an inspirational starting point to what will be one of your unique invisible journeys.

INVISIBLE JOURNEY MEDITATION

By living in the moment, you gently move towards a serene deep understanding – a "knowing"

Imagine you are in a country lane. Walking slowly, you effortlessly place one foot in front of the other. You feel weightless. You sense the vibration of the countryside. You inhale the mixed fragrance of abundant fauna. You sense the height, density and energy of the hedges and trees: the buzz of bees, the gentl, incessant hum of numerous insects busy with a purpose. You inhale with immense joy the heady aroma of wild flowers – the elderflower, dog rose, clover and lady's slipper. You sense the vibrancy and intensity of colour, the pulse of small mammals hiding beneath the undergrowth patiently waiting to emerge when you have passed by. Your conscious and unconscious mind is at ease, enjoying this wonderful experience.

You consciously absorb the vibrant energy surrounding you, discovering for the first time with utter amazement the diversification of growth, the species of grasses and fauna surviving with strength and purpose beneath the hedges and trees.

You feel the warmth of the sun, bright and golden. You glance upwards at the blanket of blue sky, observing the sporadic clouds gently moving as if they are floating, creating inspirational patterns, conveying a story. You marvel at the shadows created by the sun's rays; you delight in the instinctive recognition of varying shapes. You stop for a moment, absorbing with delight and wonder this newly found experience. You feel safe, warm and aware your conscious and unconscious mind is in tune, at peace and content. You feel emotionally uplifted and empowered to journey on.

You sense a new found freedom. You glance down at your feet. Your feet are bare – your toes free to wriggle, to breathe. Your clothing is light and flowing, soft to the touch. Your skin is warm, smooth, sensitive and vibrant.

You become acutely aware of sound – a harmonious orchestral symphony of music to the ear. The leaves and branches of trees and hedges move in the breeze, the hum of insects, a chorus of bird song, the movement in the undergrowth harbouring Mother Nature's smallest creatures. As you listen, you marvel at your ability to distinguish various pitch of sound, acutely sensing energy and purpose as creatures continue their day's journey, fearlessly and proudly announcing to the world they are glad to be alive.

You look back to see how far you have travelled. You absorb the incredible balance and harmony of Mother Earth. You see her natural world festooned in a glorious colour spectacle of pure magic.

As you glance ahead, the lane seems to go on and on with no end in sight. You realise you are surrounded by rich countryside with not a building in sight. This realisation is surprisingly relaxing, welcoming, almost surreal. As your conscious and unconscious minds blend, you become aware of being enveloped in a cloak of protection, peace and serenity. You sense, in that moment, a transformation process intertwined with sharing this special moment with the industrious magical world of nature. All is peace and calm.

As you travel further down the lane, you see an old wooden five-bar gate to your left. Without hesitation, you decide to explore. You easily clamber over the gate. Once down, you stop, noticing that the field ahead appears to flow gently upwards to hills in the distance. You slowly walk through the field towards the hills, sensing with every step that your footprints will leave an imprint, disturbing some of the grasses and numerous wild flowers growing side by side in perfect harmony. Looking back, you see with delight that your footprints have not harmed the field at all. You rejoice with joy.

Your journey of exploration has begun. You skip and run, enjoying newly found freedom. You feel exhilarated and excited. You feel the sun on your skin, the wind in your hair. You twist and turn, dancing around and around, completely carefree, enjoying this wonderful uplifting moment.

Effortlessly, you climb the slope and soon reach the bottom of the hill, which leads to a beautiful woodland full of peace and calm. You see and sense the density of growth, the shafts of sunlight through the trees. You stand and gaze with wonder at the hue of colour, the heady silence, the creative magic of Mother Nature – an intoxicating energy.

You stand motionless. In that moment, you sense you are not alone and become aware of a presence near by. You turn to greet them...

Your eyes are now heavy. You feel sleepy as you gently ease into this magical spiritual world. You are safe.

Explore...

This visualised meditation will be the first of many journeys. Each meditative journey is unique to you. Some you will choose to visit many times. Some will stay in your memory for days and weeks. Some you will learn from. Some you will find emotional. Some will be exhilarating. Some will herald a reluctance to return to the material world in which we live. This respite from our frenetic material world is rejuvenating and uplifting, recharging energies, enabling us to face life's challenges with confidence and a new found self-belief.

You will be amazed where your mind will take you. You are now free to enjoy and explore a meditative state whenever you choose: an opportunity to meet with loved ones, angels and guides. Meditate for as long as it feels comfortable to you and as often as feels right.

Be patient when problem-solving in your meditative state as the desire for clarity takes a little time to master. Eventually, all will be revealed, the right answers filtering through. You may need to explore several avenues before you discover the meditation technique that works best for you. You can go on your chosen journey at any time.

Enjoy!

Meditative Aids	Tools For Achieving A Meditative State Of Mind
The Breath	Focus on each in-breath and out-breath until a gentle pattern is achieved. Continue to focus on the rhythmic pattern of inward and outward breath until a relaxed breathing state is achieved and comfortable.
Spoken Word	The vibration and dulcet tones of the spoken word verbalised softly with conviction and passion is assimilated by the conscious and unconscious mind. A relaxing focus for an unfolding story.
Music	Sound waves and vibration help to clear the conscious and unconscious minds of intrusive thoughts. Relaxes the body. Creates energy waves of balance and harmony.
Mantra	Repetition of single sound or phrase spoken out loud or repeated silently. Blocks intrusive thoughts from the conscious mind. An affirmation of intent, drawing into focus a desire for peace and change, creating a heightened sense of awareness.
Candlelight	Gaze and concentrate on the flame until a gentle breathing rhythm is achieved. Focus until the eyes become heavy and close. Inspirational. Reassuring and calming. A soporific focus for creating peace and upliftment.
Crystal, Pebble, Flower, Jewellery, Poem or Letter	Holding an object gently between the hands, resting gently on your lap, helps the body to be focussed and still. Concentrate on the chosen object, feeling its colour, texture and shape. Sense the pulse of energy. Aids the ability to focus, to be relaxed and still.

Exercise – Meditation Journeys – Note recurring colours

Note your emotions after each meditation

_ _

_ _

_ _

_ _

_ _

_ _

_ _

_ _

_ _

_ _

_ _

_ _

_ _

_ _

_ _

_ _

_ _

_ _

Meditation Journal
Note the people you meet

Note a recurring theme

Chapter 6
Importance of Colour

How often have you awoken to a warm, sunny day, the sun streaming through the window, conscious of feeling good, jumped out of bed, welcoming the new day with optimism, the glad to be alive feeling, ready to face the day ahead? The light and warmth of sunshine brings out the best in everyone and everything. The sun's rays highlight the colour of the world – the rich hues of the countryside, enriched with luscious shades of green and brown, illustrating a magnificent vista of trees and buildings silhouetted by the morning sun. The sun dances on the warm rust of brickwork on buildings, shapes and shadows forming on the ground. The sky is bright with tints of blue enriched with fluffy balls of white cloud. The sun highlights the vibrancy of the colour in the world we live today.

Colour is pure magic, enriching our world and enhancing our visual perception of the world we live in. In essence, it is an attribute of things resulting from light reflected or emitted in so far as this causes a visual sensation dependent upon its wavelengths.

Can you imagine our planet without colour? Our world would be monochrome – just shades of grey. How dull! Living in a world without colour is beyond most people's comprehension, a fact we take for granted. How many of you reading these words are really aware of the splashes of colour surrounding you in your home, your garden, your workplace, at the coast and countryside? How many of you could name all the colours of the plants and shrubs in your garden? Yet if you close your eyes and focus on your garden, your visualisation would highlight colour in a remarkable way. Colour and light is vital to feed and sustain life. How many of you believe it will always be so?

We are so blessed to be able to enjoy the varying shades of colour and often take this wonderful, colourful plane we live on for granted – the breathtaking sight of corn being harvested in the field, birds flying overhead, ready to swoop down to snatch the ears of wheat missed by the threshing machine. Then there's the vista of numerous species of trees, hedgerows brimming with concealed wildlife hidden from the inquisitive eye. Colour is beautiful, vibrant and vital to life itself and our well-being.

Unwittingly, we meet and greet people by their appearance, physical frame, complexion, personality and hair colouring. Unknowingly, people's vibration and our first impression of them are in part due to their colouring, reflecting the energy that they present to the world. The colour of their eyes, hair and skin tone are all unspoken characteristics. Colour also permeates through their personality and disposition.

Have you ever referred to someone as being sunny, moody, sad or tired? The old sayings such as "black mood" or "feeling blue" are truly descriptive. The aura of light surrounding every living form is a blending of energies emanating who we are. Could you describe a person without referring to their colour?

Colour and the influence of colour on our lives is fast becoming a study in its own right. Colour therapists are trained to advise on the most advantageous colours to use in the workplace to promote productivity and harmony. They can be consulted on the best wardrobe colour co-ordination to complement individual hair colouring. They recommend the perfect cosmetic colour shades to wear to highlight the colour of the eyes, enhancing the skin tone to promote a healthy glow. The confidence we exude when we look and feel good is based on complementing our natural colouring. The colours we choose to wear plus our personal perception of how we feel colour interacts with our personality. Some colours encourage us to be energetic, inspirational and alive while others tend to make us feel disorientated and negative. Our need to feel positive and look good is based on our individual perceptive interaction with colour.

The colour range of cosmetics, wardrobe and accessories purchased by people born in the Caribbean is in complete contrast to the preferred colour choice of people born in Scandinavia. In part, this is due to the diversity of their natural colouring. Manufacturers like to group us together by our colouring, to slot us, by colour association, into a specific box as designated by cosmetic houses, who insert in the box varying shades of colour as suggested by their colour therapists. The proven complementary shades of colour highlights and enhances groups of skin tone and hair colouring. A clever range and mix of irresistible colour themes are grouped together to ease the choice for prospective customers. Our increasing desire to look and feel good and beautiful at all times is based on clever tabloid and media marketing and advertising perpetuating this desire.

I am a natural redhead, which I now accept and love, but hated when I was young. As a child, I found it very difficult to understand why I felt singled out. I now understand it was purely due to my hair colouring because I was different. Looking back, I was blessed for I remember happy times with some very good close friends. Name-calling can be quite horrid. I now have an instinctive empathy with young children with red hair and always make a point of addressing them, reiterating how special and lucky they are to have such pretty hair. I now accept with grace that autumn shades are best for me to wear and complement my colouring.

Department stores and superstores use colour in a very clever way. Colour co-ordinated product packaging, store décor and staff uniforms all create an image of being comfortable to lull customers into a relaxed state of spending. How often have you gone shopping with a list and stuck rigidly to it? When next you visit your supermarket, notice the colours used at the end of the aisles. Some are chosen to speed movement through an area while others create a soporific effect, encouraging us to linger, creating the psychological desire "I need." Unbeknown to us, we are responding to colour and the message it portrays.

Clever use of colour also makes us susceptible to the atmosphere of shopping malls and buildings, where again we find ourselves completely unaware of the impact it has on day-to-day living. Notice that hospitals, clinics, dentists and GP surgeries tend to choose soft pastel shades to create an ambience of professionalism, trust and relaxation. We respond accordingly.

You may have heard the expression "easy on the eye" referring to a garden or home appearing welcoming and rich in warmth, the use of a subtle blend of colours creating a harmonious and welcoming balance. Colour is vital to our general well being, but sadly few are aware of the significance of colour and the impact it has on our lives. The correct choice of colour can uplift, transform and create the ambience we are aiming to achieve, especially in our homes, again a reflection of our true selves.

A neglected home is drab, depressing and unwelcome, reflecting the lack of care, love and light. The frenzied desire for decorating and refurbishment has fired a need for change, reinforcing the psychological search for harmony, resulting in pride and achievement. Many gardening and DIY superstores and media programmes have opened up a world of creativity and expression which is available to all.

An overgrown neglected garden is depressing to the naked eye, viewing shrubs, plants and wildlife struggling to survive. Vision, enthusiasm, love and light will easily transform the garden, reflecting the care and passion bestowed. Trees and shrubs begin to thrive and intermingle. A forlorn area of space is opened up to sunlight with soil able to breath, wildlife and plants returning to their full glory. A garden lovingly restored is a joy to see.

The colours we wear reflect who we are, our inner world unknowingly presenting to the outside world how we truly feel. Many may not be aware of the psychological impact the choice of colours to wear has, but which reveals a clear illustration of our true persona at that point in time. We tend to wear dark, dull colours when we choose to disappear into the background, preferring not to be noticed, especially when our energy stores are low. By the same token, we choose to wear vibrant, bright colours when we wish to be seen, illustrating our zest for life, promoting a flamboyant confidence to the outside world.

Colour has now become part of our every day descriptive language:

"Red in the face"   *"Anger coloured her judgement"*
"Feeling tired and blue"   *"Feeling off colour"*
"Green with envy"   *"Black mood"*

The awareness and importance of colour unwittingly reflects the psychology of our doing and thinking, our zest and enthusiasm for life. The impact colour has on our general demeanour is not new, being explored and exploited throughout eons of time.

Colour and its influence on people of all walks of life have been ingrained in many cultures and communities throughout the whole world. Mayans, Egyptians, Venetians, Romans and Greeks used the full expression of colour to emphasis power, flamboyance, awe and passion in their architecture, community design, dress code and lifestyle. Sadly, some cultures and their societies have been lost in the mists of time, though their legacy of lifestyle still lives on in sculpture, paintings and artefacts. From time to time, historians and archaeologists excitedly discover hidden caves, disintegrating temples and the like releasing precious secrets to the testament of colour in a bygone age. The cultural knowledge and message of colour passed down from generation to generation still plays a huge part in religious and significant ceremonies today.

Some cultures choose to adorn their bodies with colourful body paints, tattoos and jewellery, signalling status and hierarchy in the community. Maoris, Aborigines, Peruvians, South Americans, North Americans and recently discovered tribes living deep in newly-discovered rain forests use colour as a measure of energy, wealth and position.

Glancing at a map of the world, you may notice that the hotter the climate, the stronger and more vibrant the colours become in all life forms – the plumage of the birds; the turquoise deep blue of the sea; the vibrant coats of wildlife; the vivid, brilliant colour of plants; the abundance of colourful fruit on the trees; the brilliance and brightness of the sun in the sky.

The sun's rays radiate warmth, creating the feel-good factor which is reflected in the colourful choice of furnishings in people's homes. Picture the cultural choice of wardrobe by seemingly happy, good-natured people who relish and respect the climate they live in. Some may appear to have very little in material terms, but are immensely rich in other ways, respecting and working with the wealth of nature with all its gifts, giving in to the slow relaxed lifestyle dictated by the warmth of the sun. Colour is energy.

Our choice of colours to wear, like our taste of furnishings for our home, is very individual. Our personal choice of integrating colour and design is unique, as every individual is unique. There is not a right or wrong way to mix or blend colours. It is purely a personal expression of colour, projecting an atmosphere of harmony where we can feel safe, relaxed and comfortable.

Light is energy. A prism reflects seven beautiful bright colours – the rainbow colours. See for yourself. Hang a crystal in a sunny window and the sun will reflect these beautiful colours to dance on your wall. It is colour magic.

- Red, orange, yellow – *warm colours* – **energising**
- Blue, indigo and violet – *cool colours* – **soothing**
- Green – *most sensitive to the human eye, seeing numerous shades of light and dark* – **balancing**

The various shades and tints of colour available today in fabrics, paints and wall coverings create a mirage of different colours. You will easily assimilate when some colours blend harmoniously, being restful, calming, and soothing, while others tend to be disturbing, creating agitation. When next out shopping, make a mental note of the colour range used by various shops – hairdresser, butcher, newsagent, estate agent, boutique and supermarket. Do the colours influence you?

The world we live in is undergoing a radical complex change, many yearning for a more simplistic way of life. Many successful financiers and business tycoons are turning their backs on the manic ostentatious lifestyle – the big money, the fast pace, where pressure patterning and colourful lifestyle reign supreme. Many are now disillusioned, rejecting the message they portray in the search for a deeper meaning and purpose of life.

Introducing certain colours into our environment creates balance in every area of our life, which is sadly sometimes lacking in this fast technological age we live in. Light which contains all spectrums of colour feeds, nourishes and sustains all life forms. Being aware of the influence of colour and how we apply it to benefit our lives makes a huge impact.

Colour affects each and every one of us, irrespective of whatever level in society we find ourselves. It impacts on us in every way, physically, emotionally, mentally and spiritually, fuelling a subtle awareness and understanding for growth, spiritual insight and balance in the 21st century. Some modern visionaries now recognise the huge impact and importance colour plays in our world today.

Accept that colour is vital to us, reflecting and invigorating the essence of each and every one of us, encompassing every aspect of our life. It is vital to the progress of mankind and universal consciousness. Understanding the psychology of colour, its impact and message can enhance peace, harmony and a sense of optimism. Consequently, life takes on a different meaning.

Take advantage of the message and magic of colour. Allow the psychology of colour to work for you:

- *Enjoy the sunshine. Everyone feels happier and positive when the sun shines*
- *Feel good wearing colours that complement your skin tone, hair colouring and personality*
- *Furnish your office or working space with colourful pictures or plants to improve productivity and energy flow*
- *Furnish your home with colours reflecting your lifestyle, interests and personality, enhancing upliftment and well-being*
- *Fill your garden or window boxes with colourful plants to increase vibrant energy*
- *Allow light and nature's colours to awaken new insights of awareness*
- *Enjoy living on this wonderful colourful plane*

How sad and drab our world would be without colour!

SIGNIFICANCE OF COLOUR

All colours emit positive, negative and spiritual energy. Every image and its recollection is unique to every individual's impression.

If fifty people were asked to study a well-known painting, recalling a brief description of the image, describing it in as much detail as possible, the dominant colours used by the artist and why, very few comments would correlate. Our perception is unique. Life and its impact on us is unique. How we express what we visualise is different. Consequently, how we view colour and the meaning it portrays is unique.

My impressions:

Colour	Positive Influence	Negative Influence	Spiritual Influence
Red	Passion, Vigour, Determination, Ambition	Aggression, Arrogance, Impulsive	Energised, Life force, Strength
Pink	Loving, Caring, Approachable	Emotional, Tearful, Tense	Generous, Unconditional love, Loving
Orange	Vibrant energy, Upliftment, Visionary	Instability, Physical ailments	Inspirational, Clarity, High energy
Yellow	Optimism, Self-control	Conceit, Critical	Compassion, Wisdom
Green	Level-headed, Adaptable, Balance	Jealous, Deceit, Judgemental	Spiritual Insight, Contemplation
Blue	Revelation, Clarity, Healing, Calming	Distant, Unkind, Flippant	Creative, Artistic Intuitive, Honest
Violet/ Indigo	Devotion, Psychic gifts	Rarely shown	Spiritual teaching, Ancient knowledge
Brown	Hard working, Mental agility, Practical	Materialistic, Dogmatic, Stubborn	"Open" to life, Down to earth, Sincere
Black	Aggressive, Dominant	Depressive/ Moody, Obstructive	Consuming power, Colour clarity
White	Purity, Truthful	None known	High spiritual wisdom
Silver	Reflective, Iridescent clarity	Illusionary	Protective/Gentle, Truth from angels and guides
Gold	Rich, Impressive	Distorted impressions	Wisdom and guidance from Higher Realms

Exercise – colour
Write down the colours you feel drawn to and why

_ _

_ _

_ _

_ _

_ _

_ _

_ _

_ _

Write down the colours you tend to avoid. Ask yourself why

_ _

_ _

_ _

_ _

_ _

_ _

_ _

_ _

Colour Notes:
Keep a record of the colour change in your wardrobe. Note any life-changing situation. Note your mood. Note the month and year

_ _

_ _

_ _

_ _

_ _

_ _

_ _

_ _

_ _

_ _

_ _

_ _

_ _

_ _

_ _

_ _

_ _

Chapter 7
Significance of Symbols

An object, figure, sound or living form triggering an important significant memory associated with a person or specific event.

By now you will be aware of your newly discovered inner power, unknowingly reinforcing a need to find your own way in life, to willingly begin your unique personal journey in your quest to understand the meaning of life.

You will be able to unleash concealed gifts and knowledge as you embark on a wonderful journey of discovery, empowering you to listen to your higher self, a unique being in complete control of thoughts and feelings. You will also be a seeker of truth with the ability of being able to reflect back on how much you have achieved on your journey so far. You will sense an inner contentment to tread a newly-furrowed life path with renewed optimism, looking ahead with a renewed sense of purpose. Perhaps for the first time, you will also accept that the pathway ahead, complete with its successes and disappointments, will to a certain extent be of your own making. The difference now is that you look ahead with renewed faith and self-assurance in who you are.

On looking back at chapters of your life, you will now clearly recall missed indicators or signposts you did not recognise for what they were. Consequently, their power and meaning was ignored. You now accept and acknowledge your journey ahead will be sprinkled full of important markers in the form of symbols and signs, reinforced with synchronicity. Each reveals a hidden message of perhaps tolerance, patience, reassurance or an affirmation that a proposed choice or decision you are about to make is the right course of action.

Rest assured that the signpost message will be clearly revealed when the time is right, the message reinforced by the same symbolism in a slightly different way until its impact is recognised and acted upon. As you navigate between the signposts, it is a bit like taking part in a treasure trove puzzle game. Once you discover the formula that cracks the code, the excitement builds until you decipher the final clue.

Each symbol and signpost reveals a message specifically for you revealed in perfect timing, the right time being when you are ready to step onto your chosen path. When the moment is right, the pathway ahead will be clearly shown to you. You will then move forward with confidence, focus, conviction and trust. The symbolic meaning of colour has been already revealed to you.

We accept symbolic gestures by corporate organisations and individuals as a matter of fact, perhaps with a little indifference. However, it is still important to recognise their significance. Remember that everything happens for a reason. Once enlightenment reigns, each recognised signpost acts like a beacon of light of reassurance and vision. We just need to acknowledge the relevance, timing, influence and the message being conveyed.

Symbols for me are very profound. I unconsciously tend to mull over thoughts and ideas while driving, especially through the countryside. Many inspirational thoughts flood into my mind, even while concentrating on the road, a spark of inspiration to be revisited at a later moment in time, an embryo of an idea or thought to be scrutinised later in my own space, in my own time.

When I eventually settle on a way forward, confirmation is always there for me on the choice I have made. In that instant, I see sight of a rabbit, sitting quite alone, a clear silhouette of head and ears, completely oblivious to the noise and rush of traffic. In that split second, I feel elated as for me seeing sight of a rabbit signifies my choice or action is correct. Once again, I have received confirmation that my chosen thought pattern is right. I always say *"Thank you"* out of respect for the guidance and upliftment given from the Higher Realms. To this day, rabbits and hares are special to me, always appearing when my thought process needs corroboration. I am truly blessed, for folklore regard rabbits and hares as a sign of fertility, brightness and a new beginning.

Many believe angels, guides and helpers always leave a calling card to announce they have visited, the preferred symbol being a feather, leaf or flower. My widowed elderly father, who in his search and seeking for "What is this life really all about?" passionately believed in the existence of angels, acquired quite a collection of feathers on his mantelpiece. They were always white, and always the same shape and size. *Amazing!* He had unwavering faith in the love and guidance of angels. Their presence brought upliftment to his day.

We choose from time to time to escape from the pressured rational world we live in, choosing to enter the irrational world deep within our very being. This is a special time where we can still our mind and be in touch with our higher self while discovering and trying to make sense of the mysteries of life with all the complexities and intricacy of the world around us. It's a time of delving into the mystique of who we are, seeing perhaps for the first time the impact of colour and symbols on our life, trying to make sense of where we fit into the patterning of life, where humanity is heading and why, and questioning what is life all about.

Civilisations have always believed in the energy and power of stones, crystals, symbols and images, using them for guidance, reassurance and divination. They believed in the natural cycle of life, the passing of the seasons – when to plant crops, when to harvest and when to batten down the hatches. They reacted to the remarkable survival instinct of wildlife's sense of danger, their inbuilt knowledge of when it is safe to eat and drink, and when to take shelter.

They followed the universal natural law and gazed with awe at the constellations of the stars and planets, studying and adhering to their powerful message we call astrology. This is the study of the movement and relative positions of the planets, sun and moon interpreted in terms of human characteristics and activities, which has inspired and guided many great leaders in past civilisations.

Many cultures and groups have lived their lives by the elements of Mother Nature, heralding and respecting its unpredictable immense power. We marvel with respect and awe at the magnificent untamed power of the vast oceans, ice caps, earthquakes and volcanoes. Mother Nature has been – and always will be – in control. Despite man's technological skills and ingenuity, we are still unable to replicate or capture the intensity of the many splendid sights witnessed by humanity. In the grand scheme of life, we are tiny. To gaze upon the Northern Lights (aurora borealis) at the North Pole (aurora australis at the South Pole). To witness the breathtaking, magnificent, colourful kaleidoscope of unimaginable frenetic electrical energy, leaving a lasting impression on those who are fortunate enough to witness Mother Nature's energy at its very best.

Usually circular, mandalas are a design symbolising the universe, created with love and focus by many cultures past and present for healing and insight. Civilisations have used this form of expression with dedication and intense commitment in their search for vision and truth. Each unique mandala is created with purpose, inspiration, focus and intent. Dedicated time is set aside in creating an inspirational design, insight being revealed during the process of its creation. Dedicated inspirational time allowed the artistic creator to go within, to link with the higher self, the inspired powerful design strengthening resolve, eventually leading to insight and vision.

Those who do not practice this dedicated form of artistry do not totally understand their philosophy, energy and life path. Looking back at past, cultures we respect, admire and are enthralled at the intricacy of cultural legacies left behind. It is now – and perhaps only now – that we respect, admire and marvel at the depth and reverence of their belief system and the deep understanding of the world in which they lived. Thankfully, our earth plane is still imbued and infused with their energy and imprint.

The county of Wiltshire in England boasts many celebrated sites where the earth's energy can be truly felt by those who worship and believe in the powerful energy of Mother Earth. Many choose to stop and stay awhile to experience awesome imprints of energy abundantly ingrained in these unique significant sites. Stonehenge, located on Salisbury Plain, Wiltshire, is a prehistoric ruin constructed roughly over the period of 2500-1500 BC and is one of the most important megalithic monuments in Europe. It is believed to have had religious and astronomical purposes where Druids and believers of the earth energy worshipped the splendour and energy of Mother Nature. Thousands visit from all over the world, gazing with awe and disbelief at the ingenuity and wonder at the creation of such a purposeful and energising stone circle. Stonehenge is now a protected site, safe in the care of English Heritage. Believers meet to celebrate the earth's cycle. Thousands visit to celebrate the summer solstice between 20th-23rd June every year.

The Avebury stone circle site, again in Wiltshire, is an extensive neolithic stone circle where the enormous stones tell their own story, vibrating with energy to those who choose to touch and sense. The Celtic people of the land celebrated the earth's cyclic flow by dividing the year into eight divisions, eight festivals to honour Mother Earth. Devotees still flock to revered sites to celebrate and rejoice with chanting, drumbeat, music and dance. The celebrations held at the Avebury stones are overseen by the dedicated and respected care of the Keeper of the Stones, a wise respected and knowledgeable gentleman.

Ley lines are hypothetical alignments and intersecting geographical points threading throughout Great Britain. They are believed to follow the lines of revered important prehistoric sites and tracks of ancient civilisations. They resonate powerful mystical energy created by magnetic or electrical pulses, reverberating the imprinted essence of prehistoric civilisations. Many who track and follow the path of ley lines feel empowered and revitalised by their energy.

The divination and mysticism of centuries-old divining or dowsing rods are still in use today in sourcing hidden minerals and underground reservoirs of water. This gifted expertise is extremely valuable in rural areas in Britain and throughout the world where the detection of underground streams is vital for grazing animals and land irrigation. The rods can be made from two L-shaped pieces of wire, a forked twig or small tree branch. One side of the rod or fork is held in each hand, the dowser walking purposefully in a specific direction. When water or mineral is detected, the rods cross over, creating the shape of an X. This divination method of sourcing water, mankind's most valuable commodity, has successfully been used throughout the centuries. It is referred in the Old Testament as "the rod of Aaron." This method of divination has also been known to discover coins and jewellery from past civilisations.

Majestic pyramids and sphinx dominate the Egyptian skyline. Despite past treasures being unearthed and great understanding gained of the lifestyle of ancient Egypt, the magnetism and lure of Egyptology is as strong as ever, archaeologists and historians still being compelled to excavate despite unexpected dangers. All this is done in the quest to uncover, decipher and marvel at the wealth and ingenuity of a forgotten time.

The jungles and plains of South America are slowly beginning to reveal treasures and messages of the great Inca empire, which was conquered by the Spanish in 1532. Many fragmented temples belonging to the Mayans, an American Indian people who once enjoyed an advanced civilisation, are now sadly disintegrating and overgrown, inhabited by wildlife yet revealing a testimonial to the dedication and belief system of the era.

Tourists flock to Machu Picchu, a ruined Inca city in south central Peru, which is a must for every avid traveller, who view with a breathtaking sense of disbelief a hidden valley lost in the mists of time until now the remains of a civilisation, a city so incredibly beautiful, so full of ingrained energy. The location of the lost city, hidden for thousands of years, is revealed in all its magical splendour. Visitors gasp with emotional disbelief at its immense beauty, lost for words in admiration and astonishment. The dwellers have gone, their imprint remaining, locked in a landscape of energised magical beauty – awesome! To walk around the ruined city, to sense where a lost civilisation has lived, loved and died, affects all visitors with an overwhelming reverence of admiration, respect and emotion. Machu Picchu leaves its imprint on all who visit.

Each civilised belief system has created monuments in testament and dedication of their beliefs, a desire to create, a testimonial to their culture, order and lifestyle. They executed their plans, creating designs with unquestioning devotion. Our thirst for resurrecting and understanding the past, unravelling a way of life and belief system, is still as great as ever.

CREATE YOUR OWN MANDALA

A mandala can take many forms, its purpose, creation and interpretation known only to the artistic talent of the creator. Although the tools and components used may vary, the intent is the same – an inspirational desire to focus on the inner self, to still the mind, seeking to attain a deep focus of self and the universe.

Draw a circle. In the process, focus on your inner self, your inner emotions, your wishes, your hopes and dreams for the future. Fill the circle with shapes, colours and images representing your energy and how you truly feel. While doing so, release any inhibitions. Visualise any doubts or fears being repaired and restored with newly found vibrant inspirational energy.

Allow your imagination to be free. Express your feelings. Allow your focus and intent to create wholeness, harmony, a balance in your body and mind.

A mind not at peace leads to imbalance –
a mandala can enrich and still your thought process.

Inspirational symbols have fuelled insight and ideas created by civilisations past and present. They might inspire you too.

Origin	Composition	Design
Shaman Medicine man of tribe believing only he can influence good and evil spirits pervading the world	Stones, pebbles	Medicine wheel(shape of a wheel – centre filled with stones, twigs, etc)
Navajo Indians Member of North American Indian people of Arizona, New Mexico and Utah	Sand, vines, plants, leaf and paints created by seeds and plants	Healing paintings, health, abundance, celebration
Native American Indians Inhabiting South Western USA and North Mexico	Sand, stones Woven round frame decorated with beads and feathers, colours dependent on the artist and intent	Medicine wheel mandala Dream catcher (mandala of dream world) To catch bad dreams – to imbue good dreams
Tibetan Buddhist Mahayana form of Buddhism of Tibet and Mongolia	Sand or coloured powder, herbs,crystals	Sand painting (dul-tson-kyol-khor). Once complete, it is destroyed with reverence and ceremony
Hindu and Buddhist India Title given to Gautama Siddhartha, religious teacher of N India, founder of Buddhism 563-483	Paint, sand or engraved	Mandala Decorate homes and sacred sites
Celt Group of Indo-European people inhabiting Britain, Gaul and Spain in pre-Roman times	Stone or granite	Celtic Cross Latin cross with broad ring surrounding point of intersection – a mandala
Christian A person who follows the teachings of Jesus Christ, possessing virtues of kindness, compassion and goodness	Various local stone and granite	Building for Christian worship and ceremonies. Altars and intricate coloured picturesque stained glass windows a chosen design

SYMBOLS

Symbols, the alphabet and numbers are now a big part of our every day lives. Road signs dictate the speed and measure of our journey – when to stop, wait and go. Our daily living is dominated by numbers - telephone number, house number, post code, employee number, car registration number, national health number, bank details – the list is endless. When arranging for an item to be delivered, the shop assistant will flippantly ask "Post code?" Our details are now logged onto a humungous database, available to those who have the permission, power and kudos to access. We are becoming a nation of human beings with an allocated number. Could our identity be in question?

Numerology, the study of numbers, and character analysis such as the figures in a birth date and their supposed influence on human affairs, is now recognised by many. This study is based on the theories of the Greek mathematician and philosopher Pythagoras, who believed that the order of the universe is based on mathematics. He stated that everything could be expressed in numerical form. This study is fast becoming an interest of many cultures.

You should by now be reeling with excitement at the pockets of information coming your way. Each puzzle segment placed perfectly, at the right time, enables you to draw closer to your inner world, allowing you to be in touch with your higher self. Although the world you share and are part of appears to be complex, it is, in fact, quite simplistic, everything moving at the right speed, at the right time. Once you trust the hidden symbols and codes being revealed to you, enlightenment and rejuvenation will appear.

Throughout your life, you may have wondered why there appears to be a thread of repetition, an unexplained synchronicity. A close friend remarked recently: "There are certain people whose likenesses recur throughout my life. Every few years, I meet a person who resembles them physically. I form no rapport with them and wonder what is the connection." I wonder have you experienced a similar scenario? If so, can you recall where were you living at the time and at what point in your life?

Do you ever question why some images keep recurring? For example, the sight of a particular species of bird or animal; a picture of unexplained clarity unfolding before your eyes while glancing at an impressive cloud formation in the sky; the well of emotion when marvelling with wonder at the immensity of space and mystery when staring at a vivid star configuration at nightfall.

The impact of these impressions may appear when you seek clarity over a situation, find yourself at a crossroads in life, in the middle of a difficult phase on your journey or anxious at the thought of embarking on something new. A journal may be useful to record details of when these powerful images occur as it is virtually impossible to remember in detail our impression at that point in time. Record why it left an imprint, the impact and effect it had. Write down and keep your impressions safe. Where did the symbolism occur? What is the significance? How did it make you feel? Did you feel uplifted or were you left with a feeling of foreboding? Were you happy, sad, disappointed or elated? You may ask, "What is the significance?" In time, you will decipher whether the spiritual signal or message is of reassurance or clarity. You also at this point in time need to ask yourself, "Does the symbol seem familiar?" You may have chosen it to be your special signpost prior to your birth on Mother Earth.

Symbols are part of us and our world. We need to be vigilant to note their timing and imagery in order to gain a deeper understanding. Sadly, at one time or another, we have all loved and lost a devoted pet where a unique bond of unconditional love was forged. The imprint of devotion, personality and characteristics are never far away from our thoughts, especially when we see sight of a creature resembling the loved one now passed over. Their love and imprint always remain with us. This is why we are drawn again and again to pets of a similar colouring and breed. Although we can never replicate our beloved pet, the image resurrects memories, a degree of consolation and tears of emotion to the surface. Rest assured, for the essence of their existence is never far away.

When listening to friends, family, colleagues or seeing sight of a cow or horse in a field, you may be aware of symbols associated with that person coming into your mind's eye. What do they signify? The interpretation is privy to you and you alone. The symbolic meaning of an image is personal only to you. No two people will recognise the same symbol and its significance. Remember that you are unique!

In time, understanding the message of each shape and colour will empower you, allowing you to draw closer to a place of inner peace. Your perception of life and situations will change; you will perceive the world with an original and fresh approach. You will see the best in all things. You will be able to instinctively highlight the negative and positive in any situation, now acutely aware that there is always a positive to every negative. Your approach to life will be a new experience, one of wonder and exhilaration.

Symbolism is as powerful today as it always has been. Look closely at the bark of trees, the fascinating intricacy. Touch the branch and trunk, and sense and feel its immense energy source. Stand with your back to the tree and absorb its strength and energy. Look, marvel and study with care, noting the complex shapes, recurring texture and patterns in the fungus, moisture droplets and the continuous path of busy insects. What does the image reveal to you? By beginning to perceive and understand a new way of looking at the world, you can make changes in your life, unlocking the key to inner knowledge.

In simplistic terms, a repeated symbol creates a mental picture, linking into an associated idea locked deep within your memory, triggering an explosion of imagination.

Eureka! Message received and understood.

SYMBOLS – BASIC INTERPRETATION

Symbol	Shape	Meaning
Rainbow	Bow-shaped display of spectrum of colour in sky created by refraction and reflection of light	Joyous wish. Illusory sign of dreams and good fortune. unfolding.Chance of finding fabled gold. Uplifting. Magical sign of the elementals.
Circle	Closed plain curve, each point equidistant from a given fixed point.	Completion. Eternity. Never-ending. On-going. Seamless.
Lines	Straight or curved. Continuous trace.	Symbolism of pressure and length of line. Soft = indecisive. Heavy = repressive. Short = expressive. Long = protracted. Thick = dictatorial.
Cross	Two intersecting lines at right angles to one another.	Choice. Indecision. Opposing directions.Faith. Trust. Truth.
Spiral	Curve lying on cone or cylinder with upward twisting motion.	Change. Winding path. Growth. Intricate.
Crescent	Curved shape of moon in first or last quarter.	Illusion. Intuition. Irrational thinking. Fantasy.
Triangle	Three-sided polygon classified by three equal angles.	Representing three-sided aspects of situation. Trinity linking mind, body and spirit.
Square	Four equal sides joined together.	Balance. Solid. Strong foundation. Strength. Restricting.
Star	Polygon with many points.	Hope. Universal energy. Wonder. Inspirational brightness. Optimism
Mandala	A unique picture enclosed in a circle of colour. Created with sand, stones, paint, etc.	Inspirational energy. Circle of life. Focussed creative pattern, depicting struggles of inner self. Instilling focus, quietening the mind.
Pyramid	Square base with four sloping triangular sides. Mirroring a star constellation	Mystical. Spiritual. Magnetic.Shape of good fortune.

NUMBERS – BASIC MEANING

Number	Interpretation–Positive	Interpretation–Negative	Interpretation–Spiritual
One (Sun)	Independent. Optimist. Strong willed.Ambitious.	Self-centred. Dominant. Ruthless. Stubborn.	New start, new cycle. Renewed energy.Newly ignited courage. Peace. Optimism.
Two (Moon)	Gentle.Passive. Dreamer. Inventive.	Changeable.Low self-esteem.Over-sensitive.	Intuitive energy.Spiritual awareness.Momentum of balance and harmony.
Three (Jupiter)	Energetic. Disciplined. Talented. Perfectionist.	Proud. Controlling. Independent.	Reflecting on past with insight and purpose. Acknowledging, celebrating achievements and challenges.
Four (Uranus)	Steady.Practical. Consistent. Determined.	Rebellious. Unconventional. Resistant to change.	Renewed patience and adaptability. Accepting matters as they truly are. Ability to go with the flow of events and energy.
Five (Mercury)	Lively.Sensual. Perceptive.Witty.	Irrational. Impulsive. Inconsistent. Nervy	Grounded. In tune with senses for self and others. Adaptable, accepting changes dictated by circumstances.
Six (Venus)	Idealistic. Reliable. Trustworthy. Selfless. Romantic.	Obstinate. Easily led.Weak-willed.	Open. Wholeness. Inspirational energy for self and others. Balance. Spirituality. Accepting gift of sixth sense.
Seven (Neptune)	Wisdom. Philosophical. Dynamic.	Introvert. Restless. Pessimist.	In-depth psychic energy. Deeply intuitive.Visionary. Trusting.Channelled inspiration.
Eight (Saturn)	Willpower. Intense.Deep. Decisive	Difficult. Contradictory. Judgemental. Unimaginative.	Action. Changes set in motion by self and spiritual guidance. Courage. Acceptance of change. Harmony of body and soul.
Nine (Mars)	Determination. Courage.Brilliant.	Prone to struggles.Re-evaluating views. Lethargic. Lazy.	Welcoming endings and beginnings. Seeking balance - mental, spiritual, physical and emotional.
Ten (Pluto)	One and zero added together = 1, a new cycle	Reflecting ongoing changes within cycle.	Moving forward, achieving balance and in-depth understanding of self.

Astrology and numerology is a science in its own right.

Below is a brief overview of the planetary influence on basic numbers and the interpreted impact the combination has on human characteristics and affairs.

Astrological Planet	Planetary Influence
Sun	**Source of life** – Influences energetic, optimistic personality. Original thinker. Leader. Conscious of healthy living. Lover of dance and music. Artistic. Positive influence on others.
Moon	**Mirror of life** - Illusionary influence. Changeable. Mood swings. Can distort true reflection of life. Influences female cycle. Powerful. Magnetic. Reveals unconscious hidden memories.
Jupiter	**Philosopher** – Desire to search and seek knowledge and truth. Enjoys change. Adventurous. Strong religious beliefs. Desire to understand and experience different cultural lifestyles. Seeks travel. Risk taker.
Uranus	**Awakener** - Seeker of truth. Seeks change and a challenge. Revels in the unexpected. Strong-willed. Revolutionary. Independent and unconventional. Intelligent. An enigma.
Mercury	**Messenger** – Deep thinker. Communicates with truth and clarity. Quick witted. Emotional. Mysterious. Easily blends the conscious and unconscious mind. Intellectual. Creative in spoken and written word.
Venus	**Goddess of love** – Gentle. Sensual. Sociable. Caring. Empathic. Home lover. Harmonious. Elegant. Hates discord, aggression and confrontation. Thrives on balance and beauty.
Neptune	**Mystic** – Psychic/spiritual energy. Imaginative. Dreamer. Visionary. Influences desire for the unusual and mysterious. Artistic. Creative. Seeker between illusion and disillusion.
Saturn	**Lawmaker** – Moral duty. Responsibility. Restrictive. Teaches from experience. Hard-working. Determined. Difficulty in dealing with unresolved emotional issues. Can be a loner. Hesitancy to trust others. Dependable.
Mars	**Warrior of action** – Decisive. Strong willpower. Brave. Seeker of action and challenge. Truthful. Honest. Thrives on responsibility. Competitive. A loyal, assertive and powerful advocate.
Pluto	**Rejuvenator** – Past life issues. Consciousness. Reincarnation. Wealth. Clarity after disruption and disorder. Visionary. Enigmatic energy. Abundance

Note: Uranus, Neptune and Pluto invisible to the ancients. They cannot be seen with the unaided eye.

Exercise - Symbols
Note recurring symbols that appear relevant to you. State why.

_ _

_ _

_ _

_ _

_ _

_ _

_ _

_ _

_ _

_ _

_ _

_ _

_ _

_ _

_ _

_ _

_ _

Symbol Notes:
Keep a record of the images that impress you. Note your emotions. Note the impact on your inner self. Note any life-changing situation.

_ _

_ _

_ _

_ _

_ _

_ _

_ _

_ _

_ _

_ _

_ _

_ _

_ _

_ _

_ _

_ _

Perception

How do you judge another human being
By the expression revealing their feelings
On the merits of their kith and kin
Or by the colour of their skin?

By the way they live and speak
A high-pitched voice or just a squeak
Small or tall, fat or thin,
Does prejudice taint the thought within?

Were the ancient Indians really red?
Do the Orientals really have to forge ahead?
Are the Chinese really wise
And the African people permanently in demise?

Are we programmed from an early age
To breed hatred and violence, ever on rampage?
Do we have to listen to others' thoughts
Rather than be aware of our inner thoughts?

Let us change the tide of hate
Fear and cruelty too palatable to take
Surely it's up to the coming generation
To save our planet from depravation

Let us breed a new philosophy
Of caring love and spirituality
To encompass people of every land
To encircle planet earth with a golden band

Chapter 8
Auras and Chakras

AURAS

The auric field is a powerful vibration, a magnetic energy light force surrounding every living form on this planet. The aura surrounding the human body reflects the colour of the chakras, the major centres of spiritual power located along the spinal column. This is made up of seven layers, the physical auric field being closest to the physical body, the outer six auric fields being levels of mental, astral, spiritual, celestial energy and attainment.

Layer	Auric Field	Signify
One	Physical auric body	Denotes health, vitality and disease.
Two	Etheric auric body – consisting of two layers	i) Replica of physical aura ii) Vibrant luminous colour energy
Three	Vital auric body	Vital life force.Dual energy system.
Four	Astral auric body	A total imprint of life's experiences, both positive and negative.
Five	Lower mental auric body	Denotes conscious intellectual level of talents and abilities.
Six	Higher mental auric body of high frequency vibration	Denotes inspirational link to universal wisdom.
Seven	Spiritual auric body	Direct link to God, the Power Source, when mind, body and spirit are one. Mastered by devotees who dedicate their life to God and universal law. Vital sustenance replenished when needed, absorbed through the crown chakra, filtering down to all vital energy centres.

The aura illuminates and reflects the colour of who we truly are. It radiates and reflects the colour in your life. It emanates from birth, intensifying in radiating energy as we grow, the physical aura being the only auric field that dies with the death of the physical frame.

The colours clearly indicate to the trained eye our emotional self, personality qualities, characteristic strengths, emotional and anxiety tendencies, relating the mark of past health issues, indicating possible health concerns. The aura clearly reveals who we truly are and how life's experiences have impacted on us so far. It reflects our life force essence and our spiritual potential, highlighting possible energy trends for the future. It is the spiritual blueprint of who we are.

**"There is a reason or sense of purpose for our very existence.
Every soul born on this earth plane is here for a purpose."**

There has been much interest and research in interpreting the auric field. Spiritual healing is a non-invasive, holistic, powerful approach. Spiritual healers, with the guidance and assistance of their guides and helpers, use the powerful colour energy to help restore healthy patterns during a healing session. Colours representing emotions change as emotional interludes in our life settle. Healers explore the patient's energies, explaining the colours they see and why they will be working with specific colours during the healing. The peace and well-being patients feel after receiving healing usually makes them receptive to attend again, seeking to gain a deeper understanding of how the healing energies work.

The healer may also ask the patient to spend a few moments every morning before they start the toil of the day to visualise themselves enveloped in a chosen healing colour or colours so the healing process can continue, the colour and its vibration energy being directed to where discomfort and healing needs to take place.

Auric Colour	Signifies
Pale blue light	Very healthy. Balanced. Content.
Bright blue light	Intuitive colour. Hunches. In touch with their higher self. Deep spiritual knowledge.
Purple Blue light	To be able to love and receive love. Intense emotional activity. Could indicate loss or discord in heartfelt relationship.

Auric Colour	Signifies
Green light	Change of circumstances. A life-changing experience.
Dark grey patches of light	Discomfort. Grieving. Health issues.

The aura reflects our emotions, health issues and how life's challenges have affected us. The aura truly reflects who we truly are – a vital part of who we are. Due to the thirst to seek and understand, many holistic practitioners now train to see and interpret the aura. They use this knowledge alongside other complementary and holistic therapies to gain a deeper insight into a client's health or emotional problem, which is deeply beneficial to the healing process.

Due to the surge of interest, there are now many holistic therapists throughout the world who are trained in the practice to see and interpret the human aura. Clairvoyants see this energy of light clearly around the head and shoulders of a person when demonstrating their gift. However, the ability to see the aura is not only seen by gifted spiritual people – we all have the ability. All that is required is the willingness to learn spiritual truths, the desire to see and understand, and to be shown the way forward by a trusted teacher. This is a spiritual giving, someone being willing to share spiritual matters, encouraging the student to move forward on a journey of discovery. All that is required of the student is patience and a need to search and seek with a willing desire to spend a little time in the pursuit of spiritual knowledge. Essential study or training alongside the gift of insight with a genuine desire to help others assists accurate interpretation of the auric colours.

The intricate complexity of the human body and its auric field has been a subject of study by many since the 19th century. The Kirlian camera, discovered in 1939 by the Russian Semyon Kirlian, refers to a perfected form of electro-photography to photograph and record the human aura and auric energy field of all living forms. Many have been fascinated and intrigued by this new discovery, spending time and vast sums of money in researching the benefits of this process in more depth.

You may have seen similar machines in use at psychic fairs. These elaborate portable machines are designed to take a Polaroid snapshot of a person's aura. The trained operator interprets the colours seen, advising the recipient on health trends, characteristics, impression of challenges faced, emotional scars, spiritual potential and the like. They are a snapshot in time. If you decide to have a go, you can then judge for yourself the accuracy and impact of the experience.

The size of the auric field varies, this magnetic protective shield constantly alerting you of energies surrounding you. It is your protective shield. Most surrounding energies you encounter are harmonious, so much so that you may travel through life's journey totally unaware of its powerful protection. However, you will inexplicably be alerted when you encounter energies that are not conducive to your being. You will suddenly become aware of a sensation deep within your solar plexus, a feeling you need to take note of where a sense of caution and disturbance will be felt. Your auric field is making you aware of changes in the surrounding energy flow, highlighting the need for vigilance, alerting the need for caution when encountering energies that are not beneficial and harmonious to you. You will instinctively be awakened and alert to any discomfort or awkwardness with people or a difficult situation you find yourself in.

When you next sit by the side of a like-minded person in a meditation group or at church, close your eyes and still your mind. Gently move your arms to the side of you until you meet some resistance. When you sense this, you have touched the auric field of the person sitting next to you. What do you sense? How did you feel when the two auric fields met?

When you enter a room of people, have you ever wondered why you are drawn to one side of the room rather than the other? Why did you choose to sit by the side of one person? Why are you drawn to some strangers and not others? Your higher self and aura are working in harmony, directing you to where it feels right, to where you will feel comfortable and able to express yourself freely.

Next time you find yourself standing next to a stranger, ask yourself how do you feel and what are your senses telling you about this person? Are they sad, lost, withdrawn, happy, vibrant or balanced? Just link in with your higher self, for the answers are within you.

Towards the end of a one-day workshop I held recently, after discussing chakras, colours and the auric field, we decided to experiment. Every workshop is an experiment dependent on the energies of the people attending. Those who attended were absolutely brilliant, working really hard and forging a harmonious group. The vibrations were balanced and relaxed. Everyone was content.

I asked one lady to sit on one side of the room, to close her eyes, relax and be still. The rest of the group were asked to sit opposite the chosen person a short distance away. I asked the group to concentrate on the chosen lady, focussing on her third eye (centre of her forehead) to relax, focus and wait. Initially, all they saw was a white, misty glow, but focussing more deeply, colours slowly began to emerge. They all sat for each other in turn. They saw with their own eyes each other's aura. The atmosphere was electric, the excitement infectious. They had set out on a journey of exploration and seeking, and discovered. They found this revelation "uplifting and amazing." One commented it was like "turning on a torch."

Once mastered, being able to see the auric field helps you to understand people and why they act and react as they sometimes do. Have you ever wondered why we are drawn to some people and feel comfortable, uplifted, energised and content to share thoughts and views? Glad to have had the opportunity of spending some time with them? Wishing to renew the acquaintance and to include them in your social circle? By the same token, we meet others and for some inexplicable reason are reserved, choosing to withdraw, creating a distance. This is purely due to the auric field not blending; it is your higher self signalling a warning to be careful, so take note!

Many famous artists, past and present, work on a powerful creative energy vibration. They work with an intense enthusiastic emotion and passion known only to them. They are driven to create on canvas a mirror image of the picture they see in their mind's eye. Many include the auric field in their work because that is what they see. We would refer to it as a "halo" as depicted in many famous religious masterpieces and places of worship. How remarkable is the realisation that all those centuries ago the auric field was visible to those who chose to look deep within humanity and its surrounding life form.

The vital importance of colour, its wealth of information and the powerful life force of the human auric field will always be with you on your life's path, forever interlinking with who you are.

READING AND SENSING THE AURA

Colour	Key	Basic Interpretation
Red (Mars)	Parentage.Roots. Childhood.	Essence of who you are. Energy. Enthusiasm. Ambition. Determination. Tenacity.
Orange (Sun)	Optimism.Positive. Relationships.	Sexuality. Approachable, warm and loving.Generous. Companionable.
Yellow (Mercury)	Illuminator.Intellect. Clarity.	Self-belief. Articulate. Sense of destiny. Will power. Tranquillity. Harmonious balance within.
Green (Sirius)	Balance.Nurturing. Honest.	Grounded. Guided. Sense of well-being. Healing. Supportive. Unwavering belief.Compassion.
Blue (Venus)	Communication.Healing. Sensitivity.	Serenity, love, peace and education.Angelic guidance. Meditation.
Purple	Wisdom from The Masters.	Screen of imagination. Trance meditation. Prophetic dreams, visions, grace and dignity. Clarity of events. Torch of truth.
White	Knowledge.Wisdom.	Spiritual guidance. Innocence. Enlightenment. Being at peace.

The many colour combinations and varying shades of colour reflected in the aura are numerous. Some colours tend to merge together, each pattern revealed signalling a message to the trained eye.

For example:

Yellow, blue and red – Subject's colours indicate a conflict between the pressures of the material world and spiritual understanding.

Yellow and blue merging to green – Indicates that issues need to be explored and dealt with before spiritual gifts can be developed.

CHAKRAS

The auric field and chakra energy centres are interlinked in colour intensity and energy. The chakras are likened to pools of energy, constantly spinning, visualised as force centres, "wheels of lights" believed to exist in the outer etheric of the human body.

There are seven major chakra energy centres, plus two relatively unspoken major chakras – the soul (*translucent pearl*) and divine (*translucent gold*) – to inspire, rejuvenate and recharge the soul, plus numerous minor chakra energy centres. The seven major chakras are the key energy centres of the body. Each chakra resonates to its own energy and colour relating to different vital function groups and major organs of the body. They are the life-force of the body.

The chakras, like the aura, react to the vibration and energy of the human frame. Their vibrancy and motion align with the person's energy, a life-force invisible to the naked eye. These centres burst into life at birth, the variation of colourful vibration speed and energy altering as we grow into maturity. The intensity of colour reflects who we are and how internally we approach and face life's challenges. In essence, it radiates the colour in your life. Like the physical aura, the chakras cease to exist with death of the physical frame. The intensity and importance of colour relating to the aura and chakras relay a wealth of information to the trained healer and practitioner. Remember that the powerful life-force of the human auric field and chakra centres are part of you, weaving an ever-changing magical tapestry of information. Although changing, they will always be a vital part of you as you journey on your life's path.

When the body is tense and out of balance, the energy centres can easily become blocked or distorted, creating pressure and stress on the other energy centres. The energy should be able to flow freely through the chakras from the crown chakra situated at the top of the head to the base chakra located at the base of the spine. A free flow of energy through the chakra energy centres is vital to achieving a wonderful sense of peace, natural invigoration, sense of balance and optimism. Your human frame will respond accordingly – your skin will glow, your eyes being shiny bright, and your focus and sense of purpose clearly defined.

Experienced trained healers and practitioners are trained to identify which chakra is blocked or sluggish and not functioning as it should. Through healing, they realign the chakra centres, monitoring, perhaps over a number of sessions, until a continuous flow of energy is established. This free flow of energy is essential to ensure harmonious balance of body, mind and spirit.

> "If the mind is still and at peace, the body will
> achieve a rhythmic harmonious balance."

To illustrate the point, Client "A" is suddenly faced with resolving a deep-rooted emotional problem linked to the family. The heart chakra emotions (*green*) are greatly affected and consequently out of balance. This in turn creates discord with the throat chakra communication (*blue*), interlinking with the third eye awareness (*indigo*). This disturbance now affects the flow of energy from the heart upwards and downwards, affecting the solar plexus chakra knowing/vulnerability (*yellow*), causing problems with the digestive and nervous system..

In essence, the emotional upset has created disturbance in four major chakra centres. The emotional hurt (*heart chakra*) created an inability to voice the truth (*throat chakra*) as perceived by Person "A." In consequence, this blockage clouded clarity and judgement of events (*third eye chakra*). The turbulence in the system affected the energy flow, creating disturbance in the (*solar plexus chakra*), the nervous and digestive system. Consequently, the energy flow upwards and downwards became distorted, creating imbalance.

Many people find meditation beneficial in stilling the mind, helping to balance their energy centres. They relish the opportunity to take time out from a busy schedule, to relax, be at peace and to be lost in the serenity of an inner world. Whether you choose to meditate alone or in a group, visualise the energy of the major chakras one by one as you drift into a meditation state. Feel and sense the chakras' colour and power. Visualise each chakra as a beautiful vibrant flower. Feel the flow of energy as each chakra opens in response to your own expression of ease and calm. Start with the base chakra: explore the colour, gradually moving upwards towards the crown chakra. Visualise the flow of energy as it moves upwards towards the crown chakra. Once all the chakras are open, feel the flow of energy. Allow the gentle calmness to enfold you.

Absorb the powerful energy.

Visualise revisiting each energy centre in turn, relishing with delight at the wonderful iridescent colourful flowers you have created. Then one by one, starting with the crown chakra, close each centre. Imagine the petals of your beautiful blooms closing together tight. Continue closing all chakra blooms until all the petals form a tight bud. You are now protected. Drink in the feeling of peace and calm before you move from your relaxed position to continue with the rest of your day.

This process, although simple, is effective. Time set aside for regular meditation is extremely beneficial. You have diligently opened your chakras. You have sensed peace and been in tune with your vital energy centres, gaining a deeper understanding and full expression of your own energy. Remember that it is important to close this remarkable energy flow before you completely awaken from the meditative state you find yourself in. Be still and relax for a short while before you fully awake, then slowly immerge from the cocoon of peace and light. You are now ready to face the day ahead, finding that you will deal with challenges in a seemingly effortless way.

Meditation has been and is used widely today by many cultures. If you join a meditation group, you will probably be asked to ground yourself before you embark on your meditative journey. Imagine your feet are firmly planted deep within Mother Earth, then one by one visualise opening the seven major chakras. As you do so, feel and sense their responding colour and energy.

People of the Western world are only now acknowledging the power and wonder of an incredible energy system that previous cultures have used in their everyday lives for eons of time. I have heard it asked many times, "Why do cultures of the East look so tranquil and at peace when on the surface they seemingly have so little?" Their serenity comes from a belief system heralding a deep sense of peace and contentment, something the Western world is trying hard to understand and come to terms with. We live in a frenetic material world. It is now widely accepted that everyone needs enough material wealth for day-to-day needs. The peoples of the West are slowly recognising at great cost to the individual and society that status and material acquisition alone do not create inner peace and contentment. Why not set aside some time and meditate on a regular basis? You have nothing to lose and everything to gain!

UNDERSTANDING YOUR CHAKRAS

Chakra	Colour	Location	Energy	Connection
Crown (Mediumistic) *Sahasrara*	Violet or White	Top of the head (aligned with pineal gland)	"I am a gifted visionary"	**Guided by the Higher Realms.** Spiritual inspiration and wisdom. Link to celestial beings and Ascended Masters.
Brow Intuitive imagery and imagination) *Ajna*	Purple/ Indigo	Middle of forehead	"I see"	**Gifted visionary.** Clairvoyance. Self-belief. Sight of third eye. Ears, nose and eyes.
Throat (Communication) *Visuddha*	Blue	On spine – level with the throat	"I speak"	**Empathy with others.** Nurturing, caring. Throat, thyroid, lungs, bronchial system.
Heart (Air) *Anahata*	Green	On spine – level with centre of breastbone	"I feel"	**Honest dialogue.** Ability to communicate with others – all levels. Circulatory system, heart and blood.
Solar Plexus (Fire) *Manipura*	Yellow	On spine – level with the stomach	"I can"	**Essence of YOU.** Personal power. Pancreas, liver, colon, stomach, nervous system, intestines
Sacral (Water) *Svadhistana*	Orange	Lower abdomen just below the navel	"I sense"	**Ability to achieve. Creativity.** Reproductive system. Bodily fluids. Pelvis. Fertility and sexuality.
Base (Earth) *Muladhara*	Red	Base of spine	"I am"	**Being grounded to Mother Earth.** Energy. Protector adrenal glands, kidney, spine, bone and teeth.

Italics refer to Indian Sanskrit meaning "wheel"

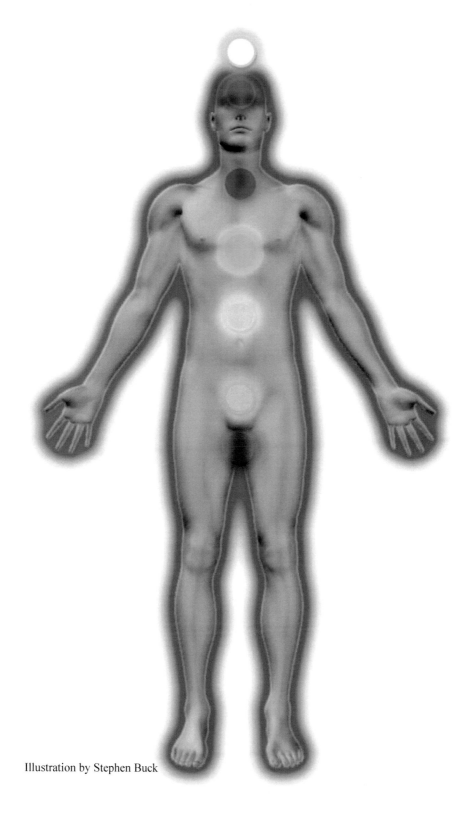

Illustration by Stephen Buck

Exercise – AURAS & CHAKRAS
Record your impressions when you meditate.
Ask yourself do you feel balanced? If not, ask yourself why.

Meditate and focus on your chakras. Note your impressions.

AURA & CHAKRA NOTES

Note any changes in your general health. Note when you feel good.
Note when you feel "out of sorts."
Are you conscious of being attuned to your energy centres?

— —

— —

— —

— —

— —

— —

— —

— —

— —

— —

— —

— —

— —

— —

— —

— —

Light Within

Everyone has a light within
Some glow bright, some glow dim
Some shine brightly all the time
Some do flicker from time to time

Some are strong, some quite weak
Strength of character, so to speak
The light shines all day long
Even when daylight hours are gone

Life does strengthen that light in some
Sending out goodness, dealing in fun
Able to share light with some in a way
That lifts them up, makes their day

A light so bright it radiates out
So bright it makes one want to shout
One wants to reach out, to share, be near
Someone so at peace and crystal clear

We can all be that light, bright and true
Yes, even me and especially you
Be content, see goodness everywhere
Count your blessings from there to here

Then like little candles we all would be
Burning brightly so one could see
Happy faces, with happy hearts
Encompassing all the love that God imparts

Chapter 9
Guides and Angels

Guide – a spiritual energy, to uplift, influence, show the way.

Those on a spiritual path implicitly believe in the influence, support and love of spiritual guides, helpers and angels. I truly believe we all have a purpose, a destiny to fulfil while on this earth plane. We are all blessed with a guide, who walks with us while treading our earth plane path. Our guide, assigned to us from birth, is close by until we pass to the Higher Realms.

Spiritual seekers refer to their "Doorkeeper." This is a spiritual being chosen to guard your gateway to the two worlds, to guide and protect you from harmful negative energies. This wise guardian is with you from your moment of arrival on Mother Earth to a predetermined time when you return to the Higher Realms. This arrangement is by mutual agreement between you and them at soul level over many, many incarnations.

A spirit guide is an entity that has been incarnated on this earth plane many, many times in order to gain knowledge and wisdom. The earth plane, as you know, can be quite a severe schoolroom. Eventually, there came a time when there was no need to return to earth to incarnate again, their mission and destiny fulfilled. However, their experience, energy, knowledge and wisdom are invaluable to us mere mortals. They have experienced first hand emotional heartache, hard labour, all the cruel rigours of living on this plane, having faced and mastered the lessons they chose to learn while on this earth plane, now choosing to be a spirit guide.

I believe a guide chooses to work with us prior to our birth. They are attracted to our energy, the spark of divine within, choosing to walk alongside us while we live on this plane. We may or may not initially sense our guide's energy or personality. However, once we find ourselves on a spiritual pathway, the energy and closeness of these guides can be felt strongly, the strength of the link dependent on our level of understanding and willingness to trust such a wondrous powerful energy.

I truly believe guides choose the soul energy they wish to grow close to and help by imparting celestial wisdom. Maybe it is because they can identify with our personality and characteristics: the blending of energies. It may well be that the lessons we choose to learn this time on earth are similar or the same as the lessons they chose to learn during their incarnation here on earth. They have walked a similar path, our footsteps in the mould of their own.

Their energy impinges upon us in many ways. They are our mentor and muse if we allow them to be. When they draw near, we may sense a change of energy vibration or see shafts of altered light, especially when we find ourselves in an awkward, uncomfortable and tense situation or danger threatens. Once we become accustomed to our guide's presence, we may find ourselves suddenly uttering words we had not planned to say, aware of a strong impression in our mind, refusing to shift our stance or go away until we have explored and dealt with the persistent impression.

Much has been written about guides. Your guide's guidance and influence is there for you. Some people place great emphasis on the nationality of *"My guide."* The perceived popularity at this moment in time seems to be North American Indians. People seem to feel comforted and elated at the thought of a North American Indian guide assigned to them; they refer to them as brave, fearless, just and wise, living in harmony with Mother Nature. Unfortunately, this sentimentally clouds the historic truth of persecution and betrayal, the sad destructive fragmentation of a cultural belief system and way of life. The vital importance of their earthly existence now lays in the wisdom and knowledge that the tribal chiefs and brave warriors share with us while accompanying us on our earth plane journey.

When a guide reveals himself to you, the mantle he chooses, whether it be male or female, will be to remind you of a previous incarnation, a lifetime where you were happy and fulfilled. This may be as a Sioux brave, Tibetan monk, Maori chief, novice nun or young fisherman from County Antrim in Ireland. The image chosen will be familiar to you, the reason behind the choice being revealed when the time is right. Rest assured that your guide is able to bring wise influences to the forefront of your mind. When the time is right, he or she may in an instant lift the veil between this world and the Higher Realms for you to gain a glimpse of what is to be or relive a moment when you were truly happy and content.

The culture and nationality of a spirit guide is of little relevance. Of vital importance are the knowledge, wisdom and energy being extended. Once the awakening of "knowing" has registered, the strength and harmony of the energies between the spirit guide and appointed soul here on earth becomes forged. Over a period of time, a bridge of trust is strengthened, encompassing a desire and willingness by the chosen soul to dedicate time to listen, to understand truths and seek great wisdom for self and his fellow man. Some people feel more comfortable in identifying their guide by name. If it helps the human soul to trust, so be it.

Looking back over the centuries, spiritual wisdom and understanding has been prevalent in many cultures – Egyptians, Greeks, Mayans, Maoris and Aboriginals to name but a few. Throughout time, wise enlightened seers stood alone, respecting and guarding their insight and belief, willingly administering healing, support and guidance to those who sought their gifted help. When these enlightened knowledgeable beings passed to the Higher Realms, they were given the choice to be a spirit guide, being assigned to a chosen soul on earth. They agreed to work with and watch over a chosen soul, someone willing to commit dedicated time to listen, learn and absorb their teaching. In agreement and understanding, the chosen soul, in humility and reverence, will, at some point, impart this wisdom for the benefit of all mankind.

People who choose to walk the spiritual path eventually know and accept their guide's influence on their life. They sense when their guide draws near by a sudden change in temperature, which can be inexplicably very hot or very cold. After a period of dedicated meditation, which may take weeks, months or sometimes years, an alliance of trust is forged whereby together they work powerfully within an encompassing blend of harmony and truth.

Once a bond of trust is forged, it is never broken. Your guide will ask helpers to assist when extra help and energy is required. They will imbue you with extra energy when moving through a delicate or extremely difficult, turbulent phase in your life by calming frenetic energy, instilling a cloak of calm, and courage and peace on a troubled mind. A helper may be a loved one who has passed over to the Higher Realms. It may be a beloved grandfather, aunt, mother, father or sibling, someone who loved and knew you well, or a spirit helper whose influential energy is paramount at certain times in our lives to comfort and support.

We are spirit within a physical frame. We are programmed by visual perception to recognise the essence of a person in an instant by their colouring, mannerisms and energy. In just a nanosecond, we instinctively accept the numerous facets that make up just one human being.

Guides are there for us. We just need to allow them to be our friend, to trust their wisdom and guidance. I liken them to being a magnificent friendly, powerful being of light patiently waiting behind an invisible door, seeking permission to draw close. We need in our heart and head to open the door, to welcome them into our inner world and to thank them for being there. We need to acclaim their powerful wise energy, and to be gracious with humble thanks for choosing to be with us. Reaffirming we welcome their presence, we now willingly choose to listen to their wisdom, comfort and guidance.

As our understanding grows, we may move up another level on our spiritual journey, guides and helpers being very much the teacher. Those on a spiritual journey may become familiar with seeing colour, usually followed by clairvoyant images on the screen of the mind's eye, eventually becoming reassuringly accustomed to the colour vibration a guide will bring when they draw close. Their energy may also imprint on your mind an image or colour that will be meaningful to you or reveal a colour that becomes beneficial and important to you.

We need to accept and understand that guides are there to assist with our progression, to be guiding hands of our learning curve, gently lifting and assisting our journey in life. What is vital is the energy and wisdom they bring. Remember that we must take personal responsibility for our own actions. Awareness opens the link to our higher self, opening a way to set aside our conscious mind, allowing the subconscious mind to flow, highlighting spiritual truths.

Angels, the celestial ones, can be called upon to assist your guide when asked to if extra powerful energy is needed to dissipate a problem quickly. Those of a mediumistic nature, who sit quietly for their own progression or choose to help and comfort others by doing private sittings or working on the rostrum of a church or gathering, may refer to guides and helpers.

When a Spiritualist medium wishes to give an inspirational message to a member of a church congregation, they are being used as a channel, linking with their guide's power, who in turn links with the energy of a departed loved one who wishes to relay an important message to a loved one sitting in the congregation. In essence, this is three-way conversation. It proves yet again that we are all spirit in a physical frame, and as we communicate here on earth, they continue to communicate in the Higher Realms.

Some guides choose to work with a mediumistic soul who is able and willing to sit and meditate regularly, linking with the Higher Realms. Some gifted mediums choose to work in a trance state (an altered hypnotic state). The guide uses the chosen physical vehicle to relay wisdom and messages in an altered trance state. Whether the vehicle is educated or not is of no consequence. What is important is the wisdom and knowledge of the guide blending and harmonising with the humility, sincerity and dedication of the vehicle, the trance medium.

Should you choose to sit in a meditation or development group, your guide is always close by. After a few sessions, ask yourself if the group is right for you. Do you feel the energies of the people sitting with you blend? Do you sense the energies are uplifting? Your guide will let you know. It is essential for spiritual energy to balance. If it is out of kilter, in the fullness of time, the group will fragment, then re-establish. Working with like-minded people in a group setting is a lot of fun and very beneficial, especially during the early learning phase. Ask to be guided to a dedicated teacher; if it is right for you, it will happen. Once invited, silently judge for yourself the dedication, harmony and willingness of the caretaker/teacher to share knowledge with you. Ask your guide for a cloak of protection against negative energies and seek clarification to see if your decision to join this particular circle of people is right for you.

When an awareness pathway is adopted as part of everyday life, your guide's energy can draw very close, imbuing you with energy, reassurance and strength. Guides will never interfere in any decisions or choices you make, as mankind has free will to follow his chosen path. Invariably, though, if we are truly honest with ourselves, we always know when we have made a foolishly wrong choice or decision. When realisation dawns, we tend to feel heavy and despondent. We then need to take courage in both hands and decide whether to overturn our original decision.

However, once a choice is made that is beneficial and right for us, clarification is always received. Just ask your guide for confirmation. Wait a while, trust, be patient and allow a stillness to enfold you. Confirmation will come. You may have a recurring thought impinging on your mind first thing in the morning, late at night or during your sleep state. Some may regard the inspirational answer or thought as imagination. Rest assured that clarification is always given. Confirmation of your decision usually arrives shortly after choosing the preferred outcome. You will then know your chosen choice or decision is correct.

Do not question the logic because there isn't one; just trust. Your guide chose you and will never let you down. Over time, a bridge of trust and respect is born. Be comforted to know that no matter how dark your passage of life, no matter how drab or dire your circumstances, you are never alone; it is purely a difficult learning curve of life you are moving through. Your guide's wisdom will eventually reassure you when the lesson has been mastered and is behind you. Be safe in the knowledge that you will never ever have to encounter the sequence of events again. However, if you choose not to listen and act on the information imparted to you, the lesson may be presented to you again in a different way.

The joy of knowing your guide is down to the individual. This awareness is something you need to discover for yourself. Dedication, trust and patience in achieving a oneness with Spirit brings huge worthwhile rewards, strengthening and uplifting you through this incarnation.

Many a time when faced with danger or unexpected emotional distress, people have called out with a mixture of faith and fear "God, please help me!" willing an invisible force to take control, the vulnerability of humanity becoming only too apparent when faced with such unexpected daunting situations. The instinct to seek strength, calm, reassurance and guidance is natural. In fact, we are going back to our roots, our life before this incarnation on earth, recalling a brief inkling of a memory of the challenges we chose to face. This highlights an instinctive awareness our guide assigned to be with us, to soften our life's path and is never far away. So just trust with unwavering belief and quietly ask your guide for encouragement and support. Help will always be on hand.

Remember that you never ever walk alone, so accept with grace the comfort and guidance your spirit guide willingly wants to bestow upon you. Your spirit guide is a powerful energy; proffer grateful thanks when help and guidance is given. Accept your guide as a close and trusted friend. Be who you want to be. Allow your guide to draw close, to guide you, to enhance your natural gifts and to bring out the best in you.

ANGELS

Angels, groups of celestial spiritual beings, who never touch Mother Earth, their vibration being of the very finest, and attendant upon God. In medieval angelology, they are divided by rank into nine orders and regarded as "Divine messengers of God."

As children, I am sure many of you were brought up to say a prayer before falling asleep, strong in the belief that your guardian angel would surround you with love, light and protection, sleeping soundly, safe and secure in the knowledge you can snuggle down, enjoying a good night's rest until dawn breaks and sunlight peeps through a chink in the curtains. As a child, to go to bed with this reassuring knowledge strengthened a deep resolve and belief of being guided and guarded, especially if prone to nightmares or silently suspected the adult world tended to be neglectful, distant and unkind.

The angelic realms do hear our cries for help and reassurance. A personal communication from the heart directed to the celestial plane is always heard. A prayer is always answered for the good of all concerned. Although the timing of the answer is unknown, every cry for help and upliftment is heard. We all cry out for God's help at some time or another, especially when we seek strength and courage to help us make a vital decision. Remember that at our lowest point in life, celestial help is always close by. When we truly ask for guidance from the heart, we may in that moment sense an overwhelming surge of powerful uplifting energy surrounding us, being high vibrations of wondrous light energy heralding angelic power.

Many angels are assigned to care for and guide children. They gently tend their innocence with a gentle, guiding and loving hand, essential in this frenetic world in which we live. Seeing a young child reciting a prayer, eyes shut tight with hands clasped together just before falling asleep, is a very special moment for children and parents alike. A spiritual cloak of protection, reassurance and love draws close to them at nightfall and remains close by during their childhood years into maturity.

Many a child has scanned bedroom walls before drifting off to sleep in the hope that an angel would appear. Some are blessed and do see angels, eagerly relating their experience with excitement and delight. Although we may not be fortunate enough to see them with our naked eye, we sense their influence and are reassured by their presence, love and fine vibration energy.

Some recall seeing angels as one of their earliest memories – the luminance of the angelic beings, serenity and tranquillity alight on their faces, encompassed in an iridescent white or rainbow coloured light. The angelic beings form part of their every day world, a perfectly natural happening. Angels guide their thoughts and actions, and become their inspirational friend and teacher. It may only be later in life, when chatting to others, they comprehend they are the chosen ones, realisation dawning that this vibrant celestial world is not seen by everyone, but just a chosen few. These gifted people pen the influence and experience of this magical angelic world for others to marvel at and enjoy.

It is believed the angelic realms leave a memento when they visit to remind you they have called. Some leave petals, flowers or a feather. My father passionately believed in angels; their calling card to him was a small white feather. I, too, keep finding feathers in the most unexpected places – on the floor, in the garden, even in my car next to the gear stick. When I picked it up, I sat in disbelief as to how a beautiful, soft, curled white feather found itself on the floor between the seats. Amazing!

Scientists and sceptics are always seeking proof to see if God exists, alongside the etheric spiritual world. They question whether there is a place called "heaven." Do spiritual beings and angels exist? Regrettably, they will never find proof in this lifetime. This discovery awaits them when they discard their mortal frame. They will then see a wonderful spiritual world existing in another dimension. We are a world within worlds. To see Spirit, I can assure you, is an incredible experience. Once witnessed, you will never ever doubt again.

Our assigned guardian angel, plus hosts of angelic beings, are always there for us, willing and ready to support and guide us in our hour of need. We just need to trust, and to know and accept they are there when we need and ask for their help.

Many spiritual healers work with an archangel, who, together with a chosen band of angels, increases the healing energy power directed to a patient. Before beginning a healing session, dedicated healers silently and reverently pray, asking merely to be used as a pure channel for healing. Hands are gently placed, where directed, on the patient. Powerful healing energy is then channelled to the patient through the healer, encircled by a group of angels led by an archangel.

Many spiritual and psychic healers are blessed with the assistance of angels who increase the linking healing power when helping clients. Angels appear to them on a regular basis. They work with their fine vibration, energy and inspiration, absorbing and imparting information received by the archangels and angelic helpers. They work closely with the angelic beings, transmitting peace, calm and healing while helping to resolve a client's problems. The angelic presence and inspiration bestowed on the psychic and spiritual soul is of the finest essence.

Shops throughout the world sell a variety of angel cards. Some are oracle cards, the chosen card revealing a message for the day, week or month. Some packs illustrate one word and picture, suggesting you select one card for each day, at the beginning of each day, the chosen card revealing the influence needed by the recipient to enhance the day's energies.

The presence of angelic celestial beings has been with us for centuries. When visiting churches and famous religious buildings, the spiritual angelic energy and influence is clear for all to see. The magnificent ceiling of the Sistine Chapel, the chapel of the Pope in the Vatican at Rome, built for Sixtus IV, is beautifully decorated with frescoes by Michelangelo and others. The paintings are emblazoned with the beauty, colour and inspiration of celestial and angelic influence. Michelangelo, (1475-1564), was a gifted sculptor, architect and painter who many regard as being born ahead of his time. Witness with your own eyes the power, definition and wonder of his work The Last Judgement (1533-41), displaying the inspirational creativity, dedication, energy, imagination and passion of the dome of St Peter's in Rome. They are works of pure creative genius, the legacy of a gifted master craftsman. The time span stands testament to his unique insight, inspiration and belief in a wondrous spiritual and celestial world. The vision, dedication, inspiration and reverence in the celestial energy and power were widely accepted and recognised then more so than today.

The angelic influence and celestial energy now inspires the work of many young painters of all denominations and cultures, whose inspired creativity of spiritual truths is captured within their work. An artist's concept and perception of creativity alters as the spiritual and angelic realms draw close to light workers on this plane, working their celestial magic to bring humanity, peace, love and light.

Their energy and influence is all around us, their presence being to assist and support us on our earth-bound journey. All we need to do is to acknowledge their influence and seek their help. They are "Messengers of God" emanating from God, the power source. They are depicted as seraphims (higher order), cherubims (guardians of light) and archangels, whose purpose is to support the celestial spheres.

Many people of all walks of life spend years studying the hierarchy of angels. You may also have heard the phrase "light workers," referring to enlightened chosen souls incarnated to this earth plane whose sole purpose on earth is to bring light, love and healing. Their own spirit guides encourage, protect and support them, though it may be the angelic inspirational influence bringing power to their everyday lives. Remember that celestial beings do respond to our revered call for inspiration and assistance. When help is received, please graciously acknowledge their help and presence with a sincere and humble *"Thank you."*

The celestial power and influential light of angels and archangels is mentioned many times in the Bible. They exert their powerful celestial energy responding to your heartfelt call for help. If you find yourself in a dilemma over an emotional issue, a deep-seated concern, need guidance on a particular problem or simply seek a specific answer, ask for their help. They are all powerfully knowledgeable, fulfilling differing roles, so call upon the archangel whose wisdom throws a shaft of insight and influence on your life's problem. Ask with devotional invocation.

PRINCIPAL ARCHANGELS

Archangel	Colour Vibration	Influential Purpose	Devotional Invocation
Gabriel	Indigo White	Guidance Inspiration Prophecy Imagination Nurturing	Develop intuition. Seek purpose. Awaken psychic abilities. Assist with life's struggles. Completion of plans.
Michael	Blue Gold	Courage Protection Honesty Strength	Achieving goals. Legal and marital matters. Integrity. Resolving denial regarding self, family and work
Raphael	Green Deep Pink	Healing Knowledge Communication Protection	Clarity of thoughts. Patience and tolerance. Dealing with unresolved emotions, hurt and resentment
Uriel	Burnished Gold Purple	Service to others Devotion Intuition Energy Serenity Inspirational ideas	Defeating lethargy. Overcoming boredom. Lack of concentration. Unfulfilled potential. Fickle and flippant attitude. Psychic ability.
Chamuel	PinkOrange	Unconditional love Relationships Love of self and others Career change	Ability to love and be loved. Dealing with grief. Negative thinking.
Jophiel	Yellow	Wisdom Inspiration Creativity Mother Nature Patience Happiness and joy	Depression. Inability to focus. Spiritual awakening. Relieving stress/depression. Change energy patterns.
Zadkiel	Violet	Compassion Mercy Purification and cleansing	Forgive yourself and others. Anger, guilt, hate. Keep open mind. Receptive to opinions.

SUPPORTING ARCHANGELS

Archangel	Influential Role	Devotional Invocation
Raguel	Relationship harmony	Conflicts Arguments Awaken hidden emotions
Sandalphon	Reinforcing faith in God, angels, spiritual realms	Doubts and fears Faith in the future
Jeremiel	Unwavering belief in guidance from the Higher Realms	Listening to negative comments Changing direction
Metatron	Balancing energy centres Wholeness – complete picture magnified	Ability to prioritise To enjoy quiet quality time
Raziel	Highlighting symbolic information Spiritual gifts and insight	Acceptance of spiritual gifts
Haniel	Sensitivity of self and others Stilling the mind	Inability to concentrate Joy of laughter, relaxation to accept and enjoy the inner child
Azrael	Comfort Feeling of protection and peace	Distress Grief and despair

Be patient as angels will hear your invocation. Watch out for their calling card. With the naked eye, you may eventually see a shaft of coloured light to the right of your peripheral vision. Be aware of a soft floral fragrance or find a small leaf or petal, a symbol of their love and dedication.

Another very powerful spiritual symbol is to see a butterfly gently fluttering by. If so, do not be surprised if you see more than one over a short period of time, even in a room with a closed window. When you do, please acknowledge their presence with a quiet *"Thank you."* Their influence is very profound, so do not doubt. My father referred to the angels as *"his friends."*

When next you find yourself in a difficult situation requiring assistance or guidance, ask the angels for their benevolent, powerful influence, as reassurance will always be on hand.

Ask the angels to quieten your mind before attending a life-changing interview.

Ask the angels to influence your thoughts and words before a meeting with your bank.

Ask the angels for a cloak of protection on a long-distance journey.

Ask the angels to direct you to a parking space when the car park appears full.

Ask the angelic beings to bring positive energy, light and love into your life.

Ask for their guiding, reassuring influence. Give them permission to draw close to support you while walking your life's pathway on this earth plane.

Messengers Of God

We are all little messengers of God
Our pathway chosen before it's trod
To character build and learn life's lessons
To await the beckoning of God's blessings

Some learn fast, some learn slowly
Some know instinctively the way to go
Some need nurturing along life's way
Others know when to go, stop and stay

There is a path for each of us
We arrive unprepared without a fuss
We grow, we learn, we search and seek
Some are leaders strong, some quite weak

Each of us has a special role
To play as our path reaches its goal
We all have that divine spark within
Blessed spirit divine who dwells within

We learn to grow, to learn and care
To teach others, to love not fear
Nor be afraid for the life ahead
Guidance to be given each step we tread

We are only given what we can bear
In equal measure, heartache and fear
Ecstasy, love, complete adoration
A kindred spirit, complete adulation

So remember there is always a reason why
Be thankful for the sun and sky
And the blessings given when we arrive
Taking delight in all that they derive

For our pathway is chosen before it's trod
Being special messengers of God
To return to the heavens angel wing
Where understanding will be everything

Chapter 10
Power of Thought

The conscious mental process of the mind – the human faculty through which thoughts, feelings, intent and desire are assigned, creating an ability to exercise or examine a concept, opinion, idea, expectation – reflecting back in time, reaching out to the future.

The Victorians would marvel at the phenomenal pioneering growth achieved in all areas of the medical profession. They would gasp in disbelief at the tremendous progress achieved and at the delivery of high level medical care and the continuing research we expect today. All health service providers are geared to improve and maintain the quality of life now expected, especially as people approach the winter of their life.

They would struggle to understand the significant development and breakthrough of treatment for terminal illnesses: the incredible improved recovery time for patients having undergone intricate and complex heart, lung, kidney and liver transplants. The Victorians would also marvel with awe and admiration at the improvement in medical care delivered by physicians, surgeons and allied professions, who regularly surpass their expectations in formulating new ways to treat and care for patients.

A century ago, the quest for finding new avenues of intervention and techniques in their resolve to administer optimum care to humanity wasn't deemed possible. Some invasive investigations and operations are now performed as a matter of course. Some proven medical procedures which are accepted today were pure fiction, created only in an author's imagination.

Medical teams now have the ability to improvise with makeshift operating theatres, enabling operations to be performed in war-torn countries. They bring breakthrough techniques to poverty-stricken areas of the world, enabling the poor to see, the limbless to walk with prosthetic limbs, giving the uneducated an opportunity to read and write. Many dedicated groups of professionals and volunteers willingly give time, expertise and support to countries whose stricken people suffer from malnutrition, poverty and disease. Dedicated multinational teams still pursue a dream to eradicate this world from dire and debilitating health problems.

Research in all areas of the medical field is continuing. Trials, tests and numerous data are explored and funded by worldwide drug companies to improve the health and well-being of humanity. However, despite vast progress, the medical profession admit they still do not wholly understand how the mind and its thought processes connect. Although mankind is making great strides in medical care, having a deep understanding of how the human body works, the mind's thought processes and its remarkable ability to recall memories, relive past events and formulate plans for the future is one area that still remains a mystery. The mind and its thought processes are unique, as each one of us is unique. Our mind encompasses who we are, our intellect, intelligence, creativity, imagination, thoughts and desire. It is a vital link to our spirit, the essence of who we are.

The Native American Indian tribes followed their strict code of existence, living alongside Mother Nature. Their philosophy of life was based on nature's seasons, adhering to the information and coded symbols revealed to them by surrounding wildlife, weather and habitat. They adopted a code of respect and trust for all living entities, knowing that every action has a reaction. They killed for food, warmth and shelter, respecting that every living entity has a pulsating life force and purpose in the cycle of life, this being the universal law. This belief is as strong today as it was then that "What we give out in the way of kindness or unkindness is returned to us, whether it be by thought, word or deed." This is an unspoken truth.

Though their legacy of existence is deeply imprinted in the land where previous generations lived, scattered Indian tribes today still lovingly refer to previously occupied land as their homeland. Sadly, many of their beliefs and ways of life are now confined to designated areas, nominated and agreed by a league of nations, who perceive they know best. Have you ever considered the land we live on is only on loan to us from Mother Nature? We could learn greatly from the North American Indian's fervent belief in understanding Mother Nature's cycles, laws and symbols.

We reflect in amazement at past civilisations' wisdom, respect and understanding of astrology, the cosmos, the power source, the unconscious energy of mankind, the universal law. Humanity could learn much from their philosophy in supporting one another while respecting and nurturing the life of Mother Earth – "our home." Remarkably, their imprint, beliefs and energy still live on, unknowingly influencing this plane's population who live and share this frenetic world – a world we chose to live in, a world we have created.

Remember that nothing happens by chance; every purposeful situation we encounter is to a certain extent predetermined. What we imagine and see clearly in our mind's eye becomes reality. You cannot force growth; growth happens when we are ready, when the timing is right. There are two great truths – faith and trust intertwined with harmony and beauty. Allow this spiritual truth to manifest in your life and change your thinking.

Abundance is a natural universal law. We did not knowingly choose poverty in the material sense or poverty of the soul. This realisation may remind us of lost opportunities due to stubbornness, impulsiveness or an inability to listen to our higher self. Needless to say, we may still find ourselves trying to master the same lesson or refusing for whatever reason to acknowledge that a particular lesson exists. Acting on this recognition is vital in preventing a repetition of struggles, complicating an unconscious web of poverty cloaked in many guises.

Harmony and beauty is a natural state of being. Allow this energy to unfold you. Trust your guide; trust your higher self. Trust the guidance given by your higher self and move forward with your life. Happiness is found within. Peace, contentment, joy, calmness and serenity are also found within. Wisdom and answers to problems you encounter are all found within so be still and go within to find the tranquillity you seek. Guilt and fear is destructive and destroy purpose and the desire to fulfil. Thoughts can be changed. All that is needed is the desire and willingness to change – to change the perception and realisation of who you are and where you see yourself in life. If "positive thought" were everyone's keywords, the impact eventually on the consciousness of the whole world would be immense.

You can change your life by the thoughts you project. If your life is not flowing smoothly and you feel you are not treading your chosen path, change your thought pattern. This can easily be achieved by affirmations. Believe and trust you have the knowledge and support from your higher self, your unconscious mind and your guide.

An affirmation is a collection of words spoken with conviction, belief, truth and desire for change. Be conscious of your thought pattern. If you have fallen into a trap of thinking in a negative way, you will attract negativity into your life. If this is the case, your life's path may seem like a never-ending struggle, a battle you feel you will never have the chance to win. Remember that "Like attracts like," so consciously try to ensure your thoughts are positive, kind and linked to spiritual truth. If negative thinking has been your way of life, you may experience difficulty at the beginning of making the transition, but do not give up: you will accomplish the changeover! Do not be impatient or disappointed if you do not achieve results immediately. Be patient.

Do not say an affirmation followed by the thought, "I wonder if it will work?" for this is counter-productive. Affirmations work as surely as thoughts are living things. Practice is important. This conscious way of thinking is new, so it may take a little time to adjust, but once mastered is breathtaking and opens up a wonderful new perspective in all areas of your life. It reinforces trust and wisdom in your life, a belief in the essence of who you are, your guide, your God and your chosen pathway.

Awareness is a change of perception; meditation enables subtle changes to encircle you. Remember that thoughts are private, invisible to others and extremely powerful. In essence, a thought is a living thing, so be conscious of your thoughts. Thoughts are like a boomerang. They come back, so be mindful of your thoughts from now on. Thoughts make up whom we are; we manifest our life through them. If we are happy, everyone around us appears happy and content, and unknowingly we are transmitting a joyful energy. Consequently, the people we come into contact with react to the happy, positive energy field they find themselves in. Identifying our thoughts is a big step forward. There are four basic feelings which manifest physically:

- Anger — tightness in the jaw, head, fist and spine.
- Fear — tightness in shoulders, back of neck, pit of stomach, heart palpitations, dryness of mouth, sweating.
- Sadness — tightness of throat and chest, sensation of lump in the throat, choking, mouth quivering, eyes filled with tears.
- Joy — warm sensation radiating from diaphragm to all body extremities, feeling silly, lightheaded.

Strong reactions like these can be triggered by our interaction with people or a situation we find ourselves in. When you are engaging in a conversation with someone, do you really listen to the exchange of views? Can you truly say you listened to all the words spoken? If asked, could you repeat the gist of the conversation or are you one of the many people who only half listen to a spoken dialogue? Your thoughts sometimes race ahead, a reply being formulated in your mind before the exchange of words has come to an end. We are all guilty of this at some time in our lives. It may be due to your mind being cluttered with your thoughts elsewhere, creating a butterfly mind.

- Attention span fragmenting if you suspect or fear someone is angry or unhappy – *thoughts wandering.*
- Mentally comparing – "A good idea; I could do better" – *thoughts competing.*
- Sense of distrust creates a barrier, a blockage creating doubts and assumptions about how people may react to you – *thoughts judging.*
- Half listening to a mundane conversation – *thoughts dreaming of associated ideas.*
- Arrogant, egotistic speaker relating past experiences – *thoughts linking to memories of similar events.*
- Boring, long-winded, problem-solver scenario – *impatient thoughts racing prior to speaker finishing monologue.*
- Placating a pleasant, mundane speaker – verbally agreeing. *Thoughts drifting to unrelated thoughts.*

We all struggle at times to remain focussed on the circumstances we find ourselves in. Once you are honest with yourself and acknowledge which, if any, of the above may apply to you, next time you find yourself in a similar situation, struggling once again to keep your thoughts focussed, you will be aware of the instinctive pull to bring your thoughts back and focus once again on the situation in hand.

Our thought process is very, very powerful. Although very few pick up our thought patterns, our mannerisms and body language may betray our thoughts and feelings. Next time you are with someone who you find boring, be conscious of your thoughts and feelings – could your body language be reflecting your true stance?

Thoughts are so powerful they can travel the globe. The time delay impacts on how quickly you receive a response. Once a thought has been released into the ether, it is acted upon.

- Have you thought of someone and they contact you?
- Have you sensed that an unexpected relative would visit?
- Have you known who the caller is when the telephone rings?
- Have you thought of someone and you meet unexpectedly?
- Have you awoken thinking of relatives in a far distant land, receiving correspondence from them the following day?
- Have you suddenly thought of someone with concern, receiving news by phone they are poorly and in hospital?

A thought is a living vibration, an energy that can be transported in a trice. It knows no bounds.

It is universally accepted that the love bond between a mother and child is extremely powerful. A mother's love and intuition instinctively kicks in when her child is unhappy or unwell. The mother is tuning in to her child's unconscious thoughts and pleas for her to make contact. If two people are in tune with one another, a message in the form of a thought can be transmitted. The thought process is so very, very powerful, so much so that thoughts can be manifested into reality. So be careful what you think you want from now on: be certain what you wish and hope for. Be conscious of your thoughts from now on as they are a forceful transmitting energy.

Believe in your thoughts. They are real and extremely powerful, a potent invisible, vibrant, changing energy!

Believing in your thoughts magnifies the power of each thought. If your thoughts are good and true, in essence for the good and benefit of everyone involved, they can be manifested into reality. Just believe!

"I am a volunteer in a local charity shop, helping out when time allows. It is a very busy shop, selling donated bric-a-brac, clothes, electrical goods, furniture, etc. In the process of furnishing my spiritual sanctuary, which is sited at the bottom of my garden, I thought that a small, round dining table with four chairs would be ideal for when I see people.

"I woke up one morning with an inspirational thought to give a few hours to the charity shop. Among the collected furniture that morning was a small dining table, which was perfect for my needs. Once priced, I excitedly placed a reserve on it, elated my thought process was again in sparkling form.

"A few moments later, a valid comment was made by the assistant manager – 'A dining table is useless without chairs.' Crestfallen, I was tempted to remove the reserve slip, but hesitated. Within ten minutes, a lady and gentleman handed in four unwanted chairs, the colouring a perfect match. Amazing! The assistant manager stared at me in disbelief, asking, 'How did you know? How did happen?' I smiled, recognising once again that my thoughts and universal law met my needs. My waking impression was to give a few hours to the charity shop. I responded and as if my magic, my thoughts manifested into reality."

I am now so in tune with my inspirational thoughts that I do not doubt or question. I just listen, accept and act. Always keep your thoughts positive – use them in the right way for everyone's good. They exist and are powerful; allow them to transform your life. Thoughts are an amazingly powerful energy. Experience will be your teacher. Allow thoughts to unfold with a spiritual undertone. Use them to promote harmony, contentment and confidence in your life. Thoughts can also be transmitted to another person. Try this:

You are relaxing with a group of friends, waiting for a much discussed television programme to start. You are thirsty and would relish a glass of wine. Your thoughts visualise you drinking a glass of chilled Chardonnay. Within a comparatively short while, your host responds to your thoughts. An opened bottle is produced, a glass of wine given for you to enjoy.

You can change your life by the thoughts you project. If you sense your life is not following your chosen path, change your thought pattern. Be conscious of your thoughts as they need to reflect clarity and purpose.

Our chakras' vital energy centres can occasionally become blocked or out of alignment, creating a feeling of heaviness and melancholy. This can be due to many factors, such as inbuilt doubts and fears, exhaustion, emotional upset and unavoidable change in lifestyle. When you sense this has happened, try to pull back your energy towards you. Find somewhere quiet, relax and be still, and gently allow your energy stores to be replenished. Ask your guide to help and support you in your endeavour. Allow a cleansing and clearing to take place. Gradually, you will sense a change. You will feel lighter in the head and heart, and sense your energy centres being realigned, allowing a free flow of energy.

If you tend to suffer from headaches, low mood, find thoughts are muddled, lack enthusiasm for life, suffer from poor concentration, an inability to focus and seemingly facing a wall of apparent negativity on all levels of life, you need to determine why. Seek an answer! This may in part be due to a blockage of energy in the crown chakra. Once realisation dawns, the flow can be restored by an effective yet simple cleansing process. This allows the fragmented energy centres to be realigned.

This is achieved by a cleansing visualisation. You may choose to do this on a regular basis to revitalise your energy centres. The time spent on this cleansing process can be as little or as often as you wish. You may choose to revisit your visualisation on a regular basis to recapture the moment and to revel in the power of attunement. Your visualisation can be done on a regular basis when you sense your flow of energy needs recharging, any blockage being dissolved by this short cleansing process. Find somewhere quiet where you are not disturbed. Be comfortable. Relax. Close your eyes…

You feel tired, weary, seeking replenishment of energies. You visualise yourself walking close to a beautiful waterfall, sparkling crystal clear water cascading down from on high. You watch the sun's rays dancing and reflecting on the water, creating spasmodic patterns of rainbow colour. You are mesmerised at the majestic beauty, the power, peace, a need to be whom you truly are, to belong to this magnificent universe.

After further exploration, you notice a clear walkway behind the fall of water. You investigate. You disrobe, free to search and seek. You gently make your way behind the cool sheet of water. You breathe in the warm moisture and savour the refreshing droplets invigorating your skin as they softly and gently fall on the form of your body. You close your eyes and savour this newly-discovered freedom.

You slowly follow the path behind the waterfall, pausing at a centre point, realising you are standing in a natural hewn out pool of water filled with energy and warmth. You feel safe. You glance to your left and right, moving forward slightly to allow the refreshing water to cascade over your head and body. You sense the healing energy. You also sense a vibrational change, a wonderful release of negative energy. You feel alive and invigorated, sensing that your crown chakra is now clear; your thoughts are enthused with clarity.

You stand bathed in this wonderful, enjoyable cleansing process, sensing all your energy centres are now alive, pulsating with energy. You feel replenished, invigorated, energised with love, light and positive energy. When ready, you leave with harmony and peace in your head and heart, cleansed, ready to face the world.

You can repeat this process as often as you feel necessary for your life's onward journey and progression. This visualisation may take only a few moments, but is extremely powerful and may be used whenever you feel your crown chakra is blocked or needs to be revitalised. The image of the waterfall with its spiritual cleansing qualities is never far away, a special visualisation for you to visit whenever you choose. Before you fall asleep each night, just for a moment, visualise yourself whole, a perfect being in every way.

The crown chakra, which is sited at the top of the head, is the key energy centre where we receive spiritual intuition, guidance, and wisdom - the power source. When this chakra is clear, energy flows freely; we feel empowered, energised, clarity and intent manifesting in all we do. Our eyes reflect a shiny brightness, our skin exudes a healthy glow and our being is vibrant and rejuvenated. We approach the life path ahead with excitement and positive expectation. Problems seem to disappear or are easily solvable. We feel able to tap into an abundant energy source. We see our life's journey ahead in a positive light, acknowledging that life is good and we are glad to be part of it. We now know and accept we have the ability to function at optimum level; we can manifest our hopes and dreams, and drink from the well of wealth, energy and light whenever we choose.

Now your energies have been fully restored, silently thank the spiritual realms for their wisdom and energy. Ask your guides and helpers to place a cloak of protection around you. From this point on in your life, approach negative people in a simple universal spiritual way imbued with love and light. Request that any unkind thought, word or deed directed towards you from now on will be returned to the sender. The sender's conscious thought pattern will become confused and overwhelmed as the unkind thought is received back. This powerful affirmation encircles you in an invisible protective shield, leaving the unhappy originator completely bewildered. Believe me – a thought is like a boomerang. Its intent is always returned.

Spiritual thoughts are a magical embrace. The path of spiritual growth is there to follow should you choose to take it. Remember that spiritual inspirational energy always encircles you with comfort, guidance and truth. Think only with spiritual thoughts and mind.

In all aspects of your life, if you follow these words you will find guidance and wisdom available to assist you in all your endeavours. Thoughts travel around the world. If you reflect back, you will recognise these words are reality. If you look forward, you will turn them into a far greater reality. The true path to spiritual truth and freedom is through Spirit. You must always remember this.

Exercise – THOUGHTS

Explore you thoughts. Are they negative and destructive or positive and uplifting?

Have your thoughts changed? If so, what was instrumental in bringing about this change?

_ _

_ _

_ _

_ _

_ _

_ _

_ _

_ _

_ _

_ _

_ _

_ _

_ _

_ _

_ _

_ _

_ _

Realisation

Open wide ye heart and head
Accept life and its daily bread
And means of purpose to go on
So allow yourself to bend and belong

Do not be rigid in your dreams
But embrace life with all that seems
To offer the hungry soul
The pathway to reach its goal

Relax and accept each new day
With the obstacles along the way
Nothing is perfect or what it seems
Remember life's span is only a dream

A lifetime to learn to yield
To live, to love and to build
Character, personality and spiritual truth
Of the inner self that is YOU

We are all so complex in our way
So busy with life's bustle along the way
Together with anger and many regrets
Of roads not travelled, lost in haste

Life is merely a stepping-stone
Of each new facet, each new turn
A collection of blessings to be thankful for
Until we cast off our mortal coil

A time to come and be born again
To meet friends and loved ones again
To reflect and look back on our life
With joy, happiness – no strife

So enjoy each moment so dear
Be at peace, shed no more tears
For you are loved in your way
Enjoy each new moment, each new day.

Chapter 11
Patterns

An arrangement of corresponding or repeated segments or parts, creating a shape, plan, diagram or model.

During my work, I come into contact with people from all walks of life who for some inexplicable reason share one burning issue – a deep need to understand who they are. They remark that they suddenly feel slightly disorientated and out of step with life as if this questioning has suddenly crept up on them when in reality it lay beneath the surface all the time, patiently waiting for the right receptive moment to turn back time where childhood dreams and memories can be relived. Unresolved issues with siblings, family and relatives are recaptured and explored.

Sadly, they feel at a crucial emotional crossroads in their life, feeling an urgent need to explore and understand answers to burning matters before they can continue their life's journey unencumbered of guilt, doubt and fear. This inexplicable search for answers necessistates a deep desire to cast aside an unexplained invisible weight of deep-seated unhappiness. This desperate search for answers seemingly has no solid foundation yet the accustomed concealed nagging pattern "I feel out of step with life" needs to be completely explored and dissolved.

A scenario of questions:
- Why was I born into this family? I do not feel I belong. Why do I feel I have very little in common with my siblings?
- Why am I so very different in personality, aspirations and beliefs from my relatives?
- Why do I take life so seriously when the rest of my family appears to move through life effortlessly?
- Why do I feel out of step with my parents and siblings?

- Why do I feel the need to be creative and to aspire to be a sculptor and artist when none of my siblings appears to be creative?
- Why do I feel my ideas are off the wall sometimes?

I believe we are born into this world as part of one huge celestial blueprint. Our pathway is chosen before it is trodden, to character build and learn life's lessons, awaiting the beckoning of God's gifts and blessings.

We live in a world of patterns and formations existing in every area of our life. The universe is made up of matter, energy and space, formed and locked in its own unique pattern. The depth and power of this planet's mighty oceans move to an ever-changing rhythmic pattern reacting to the immense power and energy of the elements. Mother Nature creates magnificent, beautiful vistas of colour and energy alongside spontaneous, intense, violent patterns of awesome power and force, the pulse and vibration of this planet constantly reacting to the ever-changing vibratory energy flow.

All creation is made up of a series of patterns: Mother Nature creates patterns in all life forms. All plant life adapts and vibrates to a constantly changing pattern. Trees, bark, boughs, leaves, flowers, fruit and berries all reflect their individual shape, colour and design. Insects, birds, animals and all life forms live and die, evolving their own individual pattern formation.

The commencement of human life, evolving from unique, creative energy to a succession of further patterns, has created mankind as it is today. Our world – and how we visualise it – is shaped in our mind from the moment we open our eyes, where we unconsciously see and sense the vibration, colour, shape and face of the world we are born into.

Our very existence is God's creation, watching over an ever-changing pattern of energy. Our memory of events and experiences undergone in a previous lifetime is locked away in our subconscious mind, veiled from our conscious mind. From time to time, we may be given a glimpse, an insight of what was and what is yet to be, the incredible intellectual mind having the capacity to reflect back and forward with recollection, creativity and imagination tinged with warmth, compassion and understanding. It is vibrant until a crucial point in our consciousness is reached when the physical frame ceases to function and the brain shuts down – the perfect time to return home to God and to the Higher Realms infused with iridescent light.

Our unspoken need and what we unconsciously seek in this lifetime, alongside the lessons we chose to master, is first and foremost to be able to love and be loved. To find inner contentment; to be at peace with our thoughts and feelings; to be at one with our inner self. To search, seek and contemplate the meaning and purpose of life while living a lifetime on this beautiful majestic planet. To graciously offer thanks for our existence, being part of this magnificent and wonderful universe.

Our lives need to be filled with a purpose and an importance while undergoing the unique learning transformation life presents us with – to recognise, face and conquer emotional needs; to accept knowing we are all part of a great cosmic plan. Our desire to set indifference aside awakens a deep understanding and spiritual potential of who we are.

Cultural lifestyle, alongside ingrained doctrine, is the biggest impact on our belief system. Many cultures emphatically believe we live many life-spans on this earth plane in order to master many lessons. They willingly accept and fervently believe we choose to be reincarnated into this lifetime for soul growth, the soul agreeing to transmigrate to a new life form at any point of its choosing.

Astrologers, who study the movement and position of the planets in relation to human characteristic action and reaction, believe our life cycle is influenced to a certain extent by the position of the planets at the time of birth. The interpretation of the planetary patterns highlights possible character strengths and weaknesses, and the potential struggles to overcome. Through experience, they can illustrate and explain why a chosen career path is more favourable for some rather than others i.e. traveller, innovator, musician, entrepreneur, author and artist – clarifying the most auspicious timing for change in weeks, months or sometimes years. Astrologers can suggest the best time for taking risks to ensure a successful outcome, explaining in detail how a desired course of action can be accomplished despite obstacles. They can also reinforce why a desired career leaning has occurred, plus the potential for accomplishment.

Many peoples of the East, and now the West, consult and govern their lives by an astrologer's guidance and prediction. They regard this science as vital when faced with making difficult life-changing decisions. The astrological planetary positions at our time of birth give an insight into past life influences alongside a window for potential harmonious and successful trends for the future. Experienced astrologers skilfully guide us through the maze and mystery of recognising concealed gifts and talents, hidden potential we do not recognise, completely unaware that it exists.

A question posed by some is, "How can the science of astrology and its associated metaphysics have a bearing and relevance on how to be in tune with life?" More and more of us are now respecting and taking notice of this much-misunderstood truth. However, circumstances beyond our control do have an important bearing on the interpretation of success and happiness. The circumstances of your birth, your position in the family, whether you are the eldest, middle child or youngest, unknowingly has a huge influence on your life, shaping your personality and to a certain extent your perception of life, plus your ability to accept and deal with responsibility. This explains how well responsibility and duty, expectations of self and others, influence decisions and choices made, brandishing hopes and dreams for the future.

Your key qualities, talents and gifts may well have been inherited from your forbears or you might have simply chosen to fine-tune them in this lifetime. Some souls are born pure geniuses with an exceptional talent, a distinctive energy, born to fulfil a special destiny. Remember that everyone has a purpose, a destiny to fulfil. Despite the apparent chaos, there is a plan and purpose for each of us. We just need to be patient in understanding the role we agreed to fulfil. In life, there are students and teachers. You need to discover what role you selected to play, this discovery being the first part of the conundrum.

If you stop to see your family, friends and colleagues as they really are, you will note they are "human beings." People who are content just "to be," happy to fulfil the role they find themselves in, finding precious time to be still, at peace with their own thoughts and feelings, to willingly accept and wonder the splendour of the world they find themselves in. They successfully find contentment and joy in the simple things of life. On the other hand, there are "human doings" – people who are constantly on the go, always driven, always seeking the next challenge, striving for the next self-imposed goal. These people find great difficulty in being still, relaxing, switching off intellectually, physically, mentally, emotionally and spiritually from noise and the incessant hustle and bustle of life.

Mankind feels safe and secure in a family group. The interaction between family members reinforces and harnesses the ability to function, contributing to the welfare and harmony of the group. Man is not a solitary being. Contact with fellow man is essential, the need to be wanted and accepted being of paramount importance. Man perpetuates a strong desire and need to belong, to feel safe secure. Of vital importance is the ability to provide for the family group.

To strive and achieve for purely selfish reasons, "just for me," eventually becomes empty, unacceptable and motiveless, creating a sense of isolation. Achieving success on those terms tends to be cold comfort. Mankind needs a reason to strive, to reach and achieve a dream, whether to achieve status and honour for self and others or merely to transform the family's financial standing. Or to possibly connect with a self-perpetuating in-built need for success for self, to reinforce pride in others, justifying sacrifice as worthwhile. To be able to say with sheer satisfaction, "I made it!" To warmly celebrate the glory of success with family members, who share a love and honour: a togetherness enriching the joy of attainment. The culmination of this moment clarifies and reinforces all the effort, endeavour, tenacity and energy expended.

Eventually, we learn to identify with the family group we are born into or become attached to. We absorb the importance in real terms of being there for family members when needed. It is during our formative years that we firmly grasp the importance of loving and caring for one another, becoming accustomed to an awareness, a knowing recognition and understanding of the true meaning of love, affection, care, support and respect, even though at times we may experience difficulty in expressing it.

It may only be when we reach our twenties that we see life in its true colourful splendour, unconsciously searching and reaching out for a deeper meaning in life's cycle, possibly feeling a little guilty in questioning the mould that seemingly has been carved out for us. At this stage, we may also find ourselves examining our place within the family dynamics. Are we really being true to our self or could we be playing a role we feel has been scripted for us? We may even question our purpose in life, silently debating whether the pathway we are treading feels right and are we on track to fulfil our destiny?

A family framework is essential for the nurturing and grounding of our needs. It is the foundation stone of our learning, discovering who we are and uncovering the hidden lessons we chose and agreed to master. Once the flame of an enquiring mind has been lit, the search is underway until answers are found. We learn by observing others and by following their example. The family unit is our teacher of dignity, integrity, morals, behaviour, conduct, attitude and perception. All aspects of human behaviour create a visual and emotional picture of a lifestyle.

From time to time, we may experience a sense of discomfort and disquiet, especially when life seems difficult and out of our control while unknowingly searching to discover whom we truly are. We might question why, at this point in our soul's journey, do we find ourselves at this impasse? It is a time to recognise, accept and release dormant gifts and unsettled energy.

During human existence, we all move through seven cycles of our life – babyhood, childhood, pre-pubescence, adolescence, adulthood, middle age and elderly. During our formative years prior to the age of seven, we accept life as it is, busily absorbing learning patterns, soaking up all the new and exciting adventures and demands life offers. It is during this time our innocence shines and sparkles, untainted by the frenetic complicated material world – a free spirit encased in love and light, thoughts and feelings roaming free.

As we learn and move through the years, we unknowingly ignore or push to the back of our minds the inbuilt knowledge, wisdom and experiences gained in previous lifetimes. As we grow in stature, we begin to quietly recognise an inner wisdom, strength and acceptance of hidden depths, the realisation dawning of who we truly are and our potential to achieve all strongly imprinted on our psyche. We need to accept and understand that life does not present us with a series of problems, but merely challenges to master in the ongoing search of tapping into and discovering the truth of who we are.

The past can be marred by a plethora of comments, situations and events. You may see yourself as a key player or just an observer. Either way, emotions and thoughts may have been coloured or tainted. Look back at events as they really are. Take two steps back and look afar. See life as it really is. Absorb, digest, accept and move on. To struggle and doubt is a natural progression, so study what is happening to you. Do not be afraid of discovering YOU. Listen to your thoughts and feelings. Ask yourself why do you listen to others, accepting what they say as fact? Face the reality of your own experience. Be true to yourself.

Deeply ingrained patterns take form during the early years of our lives, creating a woven tapestry of impressions and emotions. Life is woven with a series of coloured threads, the intricacy and texture of the inspired design dependent on the weaver. Occasionally, threads get tangled and stitches are dropped. Consequently, the pattern becomes distorted. Rectify any lapse in concentration. Retrace and go back carefully, picking up any dropped stitches. Patiently untangle the thread, but check that the pattern is correct before adding any more coloured thread. Congratulate yourself on your recently discovered diligence and awareness. Now carry on with confidence!

We are all a consequence of our environment. Many of our traits, such as colouring, frame and height, are hereditary, DNA passed down from past generations and ancestry. It may be that at times you feel out of step with your parents and siblings in that they do not appear to understand your needs. You may be struggling to pacify a strong desire to turn your back on a safe, boring routine for excitement, adventure and challenge.

On chatting to family members while tracing your family tree, you discover in amazement a paternal great-great-grandfather ignored family controversy, acted on a spark of originality and undertook an unknown sea voyage to wherever it took him, his final destination being Australia, a little known land mass at the time. It was a continent he settled in, one where he found emotional sustenance, fulfilment and material wealth in farming.

An exceptional gift or talent may stay dormant for generations, enveloping a predetermined being on an inevitable journey of unexpected events. Family onlookers gasp in amazement at the mantle of energy, talent and insight bestowed on one of their own. This chosen being, charged with inspirational energy, fuels a desire to fulfil their destiny, this unfolding and blossoming fed by inbuilt wisdom and belief in their chosen pathway.

As incredible as it seems, no two children from the same family are alike, each being imbued with their own personality. One may be the constant recipient of comments like "You act just like your Auntie Jean!" which you might find confusing and irritating. You later discover, when delving into family archives, that some of your interests, characteristics and personality traits are similar. You both harbour a deep passion for music and dance, with an unquenchable desire to be involved with the arts and theatre. You may even find that you share similar facial characteristics.

It would seem that an exceptional child's gift flourishes best when sustained by balanced conditions, ideally where monetary concerns are not an issue. Time, emotional support and reassurance all lovingly given encourage the gift to manifest again. You might feel that you wish to carve out a specific career, which, on the surface, appears alien to family roots. This break from tradition may be due to your genes or a past life experience. What is important is to be true to yourself and to acknowledge and accept that your chosen course of action is right for you. So take courage in both hands, break free from any constraints and follow your chosen path.

Do not judge another's success or lifestyle until you have walked in their shoes. Unless you have done so, you cannot possibly imagine the pathway trodden so far. Remember we all have a destiny to fulfil. Some people are natural extroverts, born to take centre stage, while others are quite content fulfilling their purpose quietly in the background. Remember that we chose our environment as the springboard for the fears we need to conquer, and lessons to recognise and master. Each of us is unique, even if we are a twin or triplet. Although there may be striking similarities, the essence of whom we are is specific to us. We all seek to understand what makes us tick, to accept whom we are, building on individual strengths and qualities.

One of the hardest lessons is to learn not to be too dependent on others for emotional sustenance, but to rely on the divine spark within, to trust our judgement, our higher self, our guides, helpers and angels. We need courage to accept and face life as it really is in its raw state while allowing the grace of quality time to create and nurture inner peace. Also accept that no human beings behaviour and personality is perfect. If it was, there would be no point in living this lifetime.

We need to accept life as it is, complete with its insecurities, inconsistencies, hurts, unfairness and aggression. Those walking a spiritual path unwaveringly trust the loving, guiding influence of the Higher Realms. When we come into contact with people not of our mindset, who we sense can easily shake our equilibrium, momentarily visualise a cloak of protection being placed on your shoulders to unknowingly prevent them from drawing on your precious energy.

Some people unknowingly and unconsciously are drawn like a magnet to some vibrant people's vital energy power source. Some unkindly refer to these people as "psychic vampires." In a bizarre way, this is a backhanded compliment because in effect as their own energy stores are low, they are unknowingly attracted, like a moth to a flame, to share some magnetic, vibrant, pulsating energy. In effect, all they want to do is to absorb some of the vibrancy. Rest assured no harm is done. Your sixth sense will alert you when low energies are close by. Those on a spiritual path instinctively throw a cloak of protection around themselves, showering the person with low energy an abundance of love and light.

However, from time to time it is essential to set invisible boundaries to prevent too much of our life force being drained away. Also acknowledge that we are actually helping others when we allow them to stand or fall by their decisions, enabling them to take responsibility for their actions. In effect, by learning to take a back seat and allowing those we care about to do their own worrying and problem solving, we assist them in becoming stronger. Believe me – in time they will say "Thank you!"

All we need to do is to tweak our thoughts, actions and spiritual awareness – to learn to give a little, step back and then give a little more. By doing this, you are unconsciously creating a cloak of protection for yourself and in doing so enabling the other person to take charge and control of their thoughts and feelings. They will overcome negative traits far quicker if you can stand back and do not interfere with their decision-making process.

Be aware of your parents' behaviour and thought patterns, which have in part been created by their parents - your grandparents. The world we live in today would be completely incomprehensible to them. To further understand your onward journey, briefly look at the examples later in the chapter, which may be familiar to you or to someone you know well. They profoundly illustrate with breathtaking disbelief an underlying truth – that family traits and patterns do unknowingly influence why we act and react as we do. Celebrate for we are truly blessed; we are able to reflect back with clarity of thought and vision, enabling us to move onwards and upwards with confidence and self-belief.

Why does mankind have to be categorised in boxes? We are all individual human beings, proud to have our own identity. We are unique. We are proud to exhibit our character, our personality, nurturing and cherishing our hopes and dreams. In the process, we search and seek for the blueprint of destiny concealed deep within. To this effect, we chose our parents to provide us with the best possible foundation stone to build our character and personality to equip us for the lessons and destiny we agreed to fulfil prior to our arrival on Mother Earth. You may disagree and think, "I cannot believe that sentence." However, I know in the days and years to come when you reflect back on your life so far, your awareness will graciously allow you to understand how well you responded and grew in stature to the family framework you chose to belong. I am sure you would not be the person you are today without the sound nurturing and grounding you received.

Those who chose parents with the vision to allow their offspring to be a free spirit are truly blessed. They earnestly welcomed and responded to the freedom offered, allowing them to be the person they truly are. They were handed a key to find an inner strength, to pursue their aspirations and to follow their chosen path. It is far better to strive towards a goal because you chose it rather than have a target thrust upon you. We chose our early patterning to sense lessons and to find ways to master them. Some experiences are quite harsh but character build, equipping us with the strength and qualities needed to achieve our ultimate potential.

As we travel through life, we come into contact with people who appear to have achieved more than us in terms of material acquisitions, career success, achievements and those who have far less. We seem mesmerised by people who are totally spoilt, whose family dote on them and come running at the drop of a hat. A thought often crosses the mind – "I wish," "I wonder," "Why not me?" Remember that more often than not, people show to the outside world what they choose us to see. They would baulk at allowing us a glimpse of seeing the real core person harbouring doubts, fears, of lack or wanting. Most human beings master this deception beautifully.

Next time you are introduced to someone new who, on the surface appears ultra confident, displaying material success, take a moment to peep beneath the façade and explore what is not being verbalised. Graciously admire the struggles, strength and courage they endured in achieving success and reaching this point in their life. Remember that life is not all it seems. One can never assume or begin to calculate the level of courage, sacrifice or endeavour expended in success being accomplished. From this point on, greet those you meet with respect, kindness and compassion. Ignore preconceived views and allow your awareness and graciousness to look beneath the surface of their achievements.

<u>Example scenarios</u>

• Large family (two parents, five-plus children). Sibling position crucial. Responsibility thrust upon the eldest. Eldest female expected to help care for younger children. Restricted quality personal space. Finance may influence educational opportunities, crushing or damping down career hopes. Time pressure results in emotional inconsistency.
Feeling resentful and restricted

• Family (two parents, three children). Father works away. Income limited. Mother works part-time. Children support one another. Eldest – wise head; youngest – the baby. Middle child seeking role in family – flounders. Mother exhausted. Expression of affection shared sparingly.
Feeling the need to be needed and loved

• Family – (two parents, two children). Father works away. Loyal wife. Controlling mother. Ability to demonstrate love and affection to friends, not family members.
Creating feeling of being unwanted and unworthy

• Sibling rivalry – (three children). Youngest demanding due to ongoing health issues, consuming parents' time and energy. Other siblings feel neglected and misunderstood. Inability to explore emotions of resentment and frustration.
Feeling the need to find love, reassurance and recognition of worth

• Single parent – (four children). Father died young. Affection in short supply due to exhaustion of mother. Children loved and cared for. Mother respected and loved. Impact of situation reinforces helplessness of children due to inability to change events.
Creating feeling of inadequacy, need to release and explore suppressed emotions. Viewing life from negative stance

• Wealthy family – (four children). Financially secure. Pressure to conform, to emulate family success and to follow in family footsteps. Spoilt. Narrow view of world and today's society. Self-imposed expectations.
Feeling overshadowed, desperate for own identity

• Titled parents – (three children). Gender and success expectations from birth. Falling in line with family demands. Lack of tabloid and media privacy.

Pressure of performing and achieving. Restricted freedom. Seeks approval. Daunting responsibility of heritage and ancestry, continuing the bloodline.

Feeling overwhelming sense of duty and expectation

• Successful and well-known parents – (four children). Raised with parents' success and fame. Difficulty in meeting parents' assumed expectations. Media and tabloid attention inhibits privacy. Feeling inadequate. Fear of under-achieving.

Feeling of having to prove oneself

• Successful academic family – (three children). Unspoken pressure of expectation. Inability to express creative talents. Out of step with family. Not belonging.

Feeling an outsider, seeks reassurance and recognition as individual wishing to follow opposing pathway

• Dysfunctional family – (five children). Inconsistent show of affection by parents. Rows fuelled by alcohol. Respect and fear a silent partner. Anger interspersed with love and hate. Relayed mixed messages. An existence of highs and lows, interspersed with unspoken depths of despair.

Feeling need to escape, to be free

• High achiever parents – (two children). Pressure of unrealistic expectations on both siblings. Irrational behaviour by parents. Obsessive with unbeknown bullying. Concealed anxiety fuelled by untold pressure. Inability to communicate true thoughts and feelings.

Feeling helpless. A need to fulfil parents' dreams

• Abusive parents – (three children). Observer to unkindness and cruelty. Needing to be strong, courageous and resilient. The eldest natural nurturer to siblings. Needing to look beneath family dynamics to explore and understand. Feeling unwanted, unworthy and helpless.

Feeling of desire and need to escape, to get out to start afresh

• Only child – Parents over-protective. Possessive. Demonstrating high expectations of achievement. Smothering child with love, affection and material trappings. Parents unwittingly reinforce need to be grateful for existence.

Feeling the need to live up to expectations

The variables of family groups throughout the world are tremendous. Some family units, due to circumstances and inherited dynamics, find great difficulty in expressing their feelings, keeping them under lock and key. Family members are seemingly oblivious to the fact that love is vital and eternal, and helps the world go round. Observe a child who is shown true warmth, love, quality time and encouragement; it will blossom just as surely as a rosebud placed in a vase of clean, fresh water. A child left lacking appears sad, empty and unloved.

As mentioned earlier, you are unique. You are the only person who understands YOU. It can be a lonely, tough existence denying your true destiny. Have self-belief, be in touch with your higher self, explore with raw honesty unnecessary comments carelessly made by people, reflect on the circumstances at the time and examine with gentleness and courage past painful events that scored deep, crushing your spirit.

In childhood, you may remember being reassured by a treasured comforter. Many still do today. Remember in the stillness of the night, just before nightfall, feeling safe, cloaked in reassuring warmth, love and contentment, resurrecting childhood memories of peace, security and safety. The comforter may be as simple as:

- Sleeping in soft, fresh cotton sheets
- Feeling the softness of a pillowcase or dressing gown
- Sleeping with the light on
- Sleeping with the window open, hearing the elements
- Keeping a favourite cuddly toy close by
- Sucking a finger or thumb
- Snuggling down with a book before falling asleep.

As part of our personality and who we are, we all have within us the parent, adult and the child. In our quest for raw honesty, we need to explore the following:

- Do we need to put other people's needs before our own?
- Do we feel the need to constantly support others?
- Do we feel we need to meet other people's emotional needs before our own?
- Do we find it difficult to be in control of our decisions?

- Do we feel we are always on the outside looking in, feeling an observer in life rather than a player?
- Are we afraid of allowing the inner child to play?
- Are we fearful of taking centre stage?
- Do we strive for security we know is lacking?
- Do we believe we are the best?

Recognise → *acknowledge* → *accept* → *move forward*

If we can find the courage to recognise a difficult painful childhood or adolescent memory, exploring the circumstances involved, the deep hurt and heartache involved, we can move forward. In the process, we become the teacher and healer to the people instrumental in our upbringing as a child. A role reversal, you become the teacher, they the child - progression for you both. To enable us to follow our destiny unencumbered, it is important to accept and acknowledge our roots, our nurturing, safe in the knowledge we are where we are meant to be at this point of time in our life. To know and accept that we are but a mere player in a beautifully scripted play of a perfectly created plan.

We need to look deep beneath the pattern of life we find ourselves in, our roots and our learning. We also need to recognise a time when we can safely break free. Reflecting on life, there may have been times when we felt discouraged, restricted and suffocated with our creativity stifled. Now is a perfect time to look back at your life pattern, assimilating positive life-changing patterns necessary to enable you to move forward.

What is of vital importance is to recognise with raw honesty your own inner unspoken expectations of yourself. Remember – we chose our parents to help us master the lessons we agreed to learn. What, if anything, do you feel was missing from your childhood? If your childhood was idyllic, you are truly blessed. You may have been instrumental in sharing your secure happy childhood memories with close friends or colleagues, enhancing with a joyful appreciation the wealth of love experienced, reinforcing what they sadly missed.

There is a very true saying, "We do not miss what we do not have." By the same token, from time to time we observe family dynamics that clearly illustrate what was lacking in our early years. Be mindful – it is purely a small segment of a pattern of interaction with life-determining qualities of caring, compassion, respect, gentleness, reassurance, consideration and encouragement towards our fellow man.

Your past houses your God, your beginning, your parents, your siblings, your friends and yourself. Face your fears. Look forward to the future. The present is just that – a time to relish, to enjoy. You brought with you to this lifetime a treasure chest of gifts, hopes and dreams. Have the courage to say goodbye to past doubts and fears. Open your treasure chest of gifts with love, light and excitement. Be open to receive.

Exercise – PATTERN EXPLORATION
Write down and explore the lessons you feel you chose to learn as a child

In hindsight, do you feel you were the student or teacher? Explore your thinking

Guilt

Shed not a tear, for I am here
Have no fear, I am always near
To hear the sobs of guilt and grief
Pray, listen child for I bring relief

Just ask yourself, why, oh why
Do you torture yourself, oh why
Is it to punish yourself again
For the anguish of all that guilt and pain?

Look at events as they really are
Take two steps back and look afar
See the problem from a different view
On all four sides, clear and true

Remember everything has its time and place
Sadness and despair, all sent to chase
And keep us firmly on our toes
To character build for friends and foes

We blame ourselves oft too often
For situations and events need to be forgotten
Maybe because things didn't work in the way
Or we didn't have the courage to have our say

Just remember life is a stepping stone
Like sweet music, it has its tone
And a guilty cloak is heavy to wear
Dreary and dark, woven in fear

So let life's burdens fall to the ground
Give a friendly smile, put away the frown
For your life must take on a new blend
Bright new pattern, a bright new trend

Chapter 12
Clearing the Path

Removing unwanted objects and debris from road or surfaced walk

Life is a journey. Every human being treads a pathway known only to themselves, their own individual journey to complete. Irrespective of how communicative we are to our loved ones and fellow man, we hold sacred our own private thoughts, aspirations, doubts and fears. Life in essence is unique to us, beginning with conception to our moment of birth. We can all be likened to a precious magnificent gemstone before it is cut, shaped and polished.

We are bestowed with in-built qualities, plus an ability to uncover and recognise hidden gifts and talents. Inspiration awakens those willing to listen to their higher self, highlighting opportunities to develop and master the immense potential bestowed upon each and every one of us. As our understanding grows, we acknowledge, sometimes reluctantly, a propensity towards negative thoughts and feelings, which we silently know hinders our progress. Eventually life shows, by example, a need to listen to wisdom and teaching of an inner higher knowledge, enabling us to recognise truth in all its guises, imbuing us with courage to accept and discard negative influences. During this process, we unwittingly draw towards us harmonious and beneficial influences. Consciously aware, life seems smoother. Obstacles and struggles seemingly disappear.

One of our many lessons to master will be to recognise these negative leanings and willingly accept that they are responsible for draining our vital life force energy, in the process reinforcing an obstructive and destructive mindset. This awakening emphasises the stark realisation how over the years negative tendencies have restricted valuable time and precious energy. What a waste!

In the event you choose to make positive changes, preventing further deep, silent suffering and unhappiness, take courage in both hands and recognise the enormous loss of precious energy expended in pursuing negative tendencies. Rise to the challenge. Dismiss and discard perpetual pessimistic powerful thoughts and patterns that seem to dominate your thinking and your doing, encroaching upon your very being. Learn to cultivate the art of a "forgive and forget" philosophy, reinforcing a complete turnaround of attitude and perception.

With raw honesty, we may find ourselves from time to time enveloped in a chain of circumstances not of our making and abhorrent against our very being. Where we feel uncomfortable and suppressed, honest communication is nigh impossible, instigating resentment and unresolved emotional feelings. These crush our inner self, hindering our ability to progress further with our hopes and dreams. It is an acrimonious situation, one which fuels an uncontrollable, intricate whirlpool of negative emotions spiralling downwards.

We deserve and owe it to ourselves to be happy in this lifetime, to reach for our dream, and to strive and achieve our full potential. We can at times be likened to delicate meadow flowers struggling for sunlight and nourishment embedded deep within meadow grass, hidden from view amongst the subtle fragrance and colour of a field brimming with life on a warm summer's day. Some flowers and grasses, when crushed with the weight of a foot, quickly spring back to life. Others remain permanently damaged, never fully recovering from the weight of the footstep.

Be proud to be unique. Develop and nurture an independent streak. Value your identity and trust your inner guidance to find a way forward. Learn to see, listen and understand exactly what is happening around and surrounding you. Remember that everything happens for a reason; nothing happens by chance. Believe in synchronicity. Look for and be open to recognise signposts. Begin to look deep beneath the surface of the pattern of life. Listen and be conscious of your intuition. When you see a symbolic sign and it feels right to break free, be decisive. Recognise you are worthy, allowing your higher self to replenish your newly found energy. Graciously accept that we thrive when we are nurtured, loved and encouraged.

If hand on heart you truly feel your needs are not being met, reluctantly knowing support is not forthcoming from loved ones, friends or family, simply tap into the endless powerful energy within to release a hidden wealth of fortitude and determination. Ignite the flame of self-belief: know without question that you have the will and energy to strive to achieve your purpose. Accept with dignity and grace the need to leave past hurts and disappointments behind. Bravely clear your pathway ahead and look forward with renewed passion and confidence, fuelling an in-built trust of self-belief. Accept the importance of clearing past emotional imprints and scars. This is essential in revitalising dormant energies, enabling challenges to be mastered, sometimes against all odds. Discover with exhilaration the freedom and weightlessness of knowing you have discovered a way of tapping into a limitless source of power deep within.

Irrespective of age, privilege or position, we need to take personal responsibility for our thoughts, actions and reactions. Remember that each of us is a unique human being. We each have a purpose, a need to find our own path, to focus on the journey ahead with self-belief and fortitude. So take courage in both hands, be prepared to part company with doubts and fears, and with conviction replace them with a newly moulded YOU of potential brilliance to recognise and take advantage of opportunities when they arise. With new inner strength and guidance, accept it is essential on occasions to take two or three steps backwards before being able to move forward one pace. This newly found self-belief forges an indomitable strength of purpose to change direction, especially when you know deep in your heart you are heading in the wrong direction, on a possible collision course or a dead end.

Our entrance into this world is a living miracle, a wonder of creation. Many believe it to be the most difficult and traumatic journey we will make yet very, very few remember this emotional event. Our existence before life as we know it, before taking our first breath into this world, was safe and nurtured, with our needs met. Differing opinions as to when we actually come into existence rages on. We are, I believe, a spark of the divine from the moment of conception, unknowingly absorbing emotions, cares and concerns of our mother while safe in the womb. Oblivious though we may be during this gestation period, we sense and absorb energies surrounding us. As we grow, we become more and more acutely aware of circumstances affecting our mother, sensing differing vibrations, deep-seated emotions, clearly distinguishing between the pitch of calming music, harsh and soft vibration soundwaves which, unbeknown to us, may be the very start of our learning.

Every newborn baby is a wonder of existence. We all marvel at creation, the inner child within each of us coming alive, excited, in awe, when witnessing the miracle of life – the birth of a lamb, calf, foal, kitten or puppy. We instinctively become emotionally aroused, displaying deep unrecognised feelings of marvel and complete wonder.

Witnessing the birth of a new baby is an amazing and emotional event. It is an emotive experience forever lodged deep within the memory. We arrive in this world seemingly unprepared for the journey ahead, realisation eventually dawning that our pathway is chosen before it is trodden. We do not arrive in a neat packaged box, tied up with streamers and ribbon, with an accompanying instruction manual listing possible accomplishments, true potential, lessons to be mastered and pitfalls to avoid. We are not born with a guarantee tag on our toe. The pattern you find yourself in at this point in time may be uncomfortable, but has been chosen to help shape your character and personality. What is of vital importance is the fact that you are perfect in God's eyes, so be happy and content to be you.

"Inner peace and contentment is borne out of enjoying the life you have and joyfully appreciating your achievements, however small"

Reflective memories, images and imprints colour our thinking, perception and attitude. They unconsciously intertwine into our way of life, our thinking, choices and decisions: they affect who we are. Over a period of time, we sense and recognise words, phrases and events we know hinder our progress, reinforcing hidden doubts and fears. We begin to sense a hungry need to change our perception of life, perhaps for the first time seeing situations and people around us in their true colours. Remember that life is what you make it. Life is not a dress rehearsal; your existence on earth is real life. You can continue to travel life's journey in the belief you have been short-changed or with sufficient earthly means and energy to continue your journey.

A balanced approach to life is vital in all forms – physically, mentally, emotionally, intellectually and spiritually. Once achieved, balance is evident for all to see. It is noticeable in your general demeanour, your approach to potentially difficult situations, future planning, peace of mind, healthy lifestyle and your well-being. It cannot be emphasised enough the importance of walking life's path as lightly as possible. If you are a frequent traveller by aircraft, you will be aware of the luggage limit – an irritant to some, but essential to ensure the weight ratio is correct so the aircraft takes off and lands safely.

Accepting hidden painful truths is difficult. Dealing with buried issues allows a transition to take place, allowing a burnishing and polishing of the gemstone that is you. It is about deciding not to straddle two paths to please others, but to step firmly with conviction onto one, leaving the other behind, to visualise with honesty and clarity where you choose to be. Accept confrontation with a newly acquired graceful calm, especially when others seemingly try to continually manipulate and influence your actions and decisions.

Also accept that sometimes we can admire someone so much and be so mesmerised by their presence and their perceived success that we forget ourselves, unwittingly tending to live in their shadow rather than standing in our own light. Accept that we can easily allow another's powerful personality to cast a shadow over our existence, inhibiting self-belief, their influence unknowingly overshadowing our creative thoughts and visions.

During this enlightening period, it is important to set aside some quiet time to reflect on events and situations with a renewed warmth, grace and compassion, gently reminding ourselves yet again that everyone has lessons to learn and perhaps to discover we have in the past been an influential teacher rather than the student. How we respond to these revelations can be painfully overwhelming. We may have been focussing our attention on the outside world rather than on our needs and the calling of our inner self. We need to accept that some people tend to listen and respond to rubbish whereas we need to proudly present our strengths to the world while harnessing our weaknesses.

Those on a spiritual pathway continually seek answers to questions of life and its meaning, and what is the right way. Remember that the answers to all your deliberations are within. Consciously develop this rapport with your higher self. You will eventually choose to share your insight and powerful message with others, encouraging and inspiring them to follow your lead, nurturing a natural willingness by them to commence the process of searching and seeking for themselves. Accept graciously when you sense and acknowledge that time spent with others does not merit your valuable energy and sadly is not worthy and beneficial to your well-being. If so, diligently walk away. Rest assured that they will be receptive to change when the time is right for them.

Remember that struggle and doubt is a natural progression of making great conscious strides in discovering whom YOU are. Accept and note conscious changes with excitement and wonder at your spontaneous turnaround. Do not be afraid of discovering yourself. Do not listen to others, but face the reality of your own experience.

This affirmation can be used to harness the deep well of powerful energy within:

I am a spark of the divine, of God, the cosmos and universal consciousness. I know I am loved, imbued with gifts, wisdom and serenity.

I know any difficulties I face are merely challenges to overcome, knowing that the answers within will be revealed at the right time for the highest good of all concerned. I no longer have the need to dwell on anxieties or concerns knowingly or unknowingly created by others. I accept they are merely character-building blocks to be mastered with grace and optimism.

I know my needs will be met, my energy stores replenished. I accept there is a reason for every situation, with blessings I will soon understand.

I face the future with faith, trust and self-belief. I am safe in God's hand, at peace and empowered for my pathway ahead.

To some extent, our character is shaped by the culture we are born into. Our ancestral roots, country of birth, location, family dynamics, financial security or the lack of it reinforces the impressions of our early years. Choice of educational opportunities, plus inherent intellectual ability and wherewithal, opens wide a myriad of possibilities in the event we choose to pursue further study. The pursuit of a chosen career, alongside working colleagues who share the same interest and passion, contributes a reinforced strength and support for the pathway ahead. Habits cultivated throughout a lifetime incorporate memories and reactions to events impregnated from childhood, leaving a seemingly indelible imprint. The childhood years and beyond carve deeply ingrained patterns we eventually choose to explore for positive interaction and negative traits.

Find time to reflect and revisit an accepted moral code and belief system, a behaviour pattern and an accepted family diet. Reflect and deliberate family members' interaction with each other. Familial facial expressions, alongside an accepted familial way of problem solving, all leave an impressionable imprint. This process may also reveal inherent mannerisms, likes and dislikes and deep-rooted fears during examining a resurgence of habits seemingly developed over generations.

Reliving an accepted way of dealing with financial matters leads you to analyse an inherent attitude to money, support to family members or lack of it, especially when in deep distress or during an unexpected crisis. To recognise the neediness in some, triggering generation traits of being irresponsible and disruptive, with an oblivious need to be the constant centre of attention with total disregard of how others feel. To understand with crystal clear clarity why the words "should" and "ought" reverberate clanging bells, reverberating a tune of rebellious resentment, wishing for these words to be banned from the family vocabulary.

To glance back with raw honesty at your childhood and adolescent years, reliving the careless cruelty of harsh words, the tone and impact still ringing in your ears, phrases you wish you could delete forever. To remember the disapproving look from someone you respect and love, to recall how you shrivelled inside with deep hurt, reinforcing the emptiness of letting yourself and others down. This could be a painful memory you cannot easily erase from your heart and head no matter how hard you try.

In reflecting back on your life, sometimes the feelings of happiness and joy recede deep within your being, submerged by silent tears of heart-wrenching pain you just cannot eradicate, with images you cannot forget. In your low moments, you may feel immersed in a blanket of loneliness and unworthiness, regurgitating emotional smarting and hurt, remembering sometimes being forced to be the recipient of other people's guilt. Accept with grace the conscious essential need to follow one's own destiny unencumbered. It is your right to be happy, to feel safe, secure and empowered in your own skin. Accept family emotional problems as just that – belonging to the family.

It is your choice – and your choice alone – if you choose to carry on shouldering other people's responsibilities or believe you should carry their load. Remember that every family member is responsible for their contribution and interaction within the family group, however big or small. Be alert to the fact there are always two sides to every situation. You are not alone.

153

"Facing the future with determination and courage" could be a quote describing inveterate explorers. This analogy is just as important in your own life. Inevitably, throughout life we inadvertently assimilate negative emotional and psychological baggage. Some we create ourselves; some we absorb from others. Baggage may be the spoken word, an event, incident, situation or action instigated by others creating a chain of thoughts and events that painfully hurt, leaving a deep gouge on our psyche, overshadowing the essence of who we are and preventing us from achieving our full potential.

Be aware that our baggage is totally invisible to others. Only we know it exists.

We can easily become so adept at hiding sleights and hurts that we choose to forget the memory exists. Baggage can be so deeply ingrained that we choose not to recall painful incidents, seemingly finding it easier to conceal our deep heart-wrenching feelings, in truth neglecting to be who we truly are, fearing how we will react if we announce to ourselves and the world that we really do care, we do feel vulnerable at times and we need loving.

If we were truthful, we would never, ever find a suitcase big enough to contain all our accumulated baggage. If we could, would we then choose to compartmentalise our doubts and fears into sad and unhappy memories, disappointments, resentment, rejection, anger, disillusionment and emotional sleights all collected on life's journey? It is of vital importance to acknowledge and recognise that your baggage of negative hurts and imprints is completely invisible to others. An onlooker is totally unaware of the concealed weight of burden you are carrying. How can you possibly begin to share with others the load you are carrying, one which is deeply embedded within the essence of who you are?

Unfortunately, we can become so bogged down with the anxieties, stresses and strains of modern life that we can easily forget we came into this world to live, laugh and to enjoy our existence on this earth plane. We are here to richly learn from our experiences and to fulfil our potential while aiming to create our dream.

Let us suppose for a moment that every negative unhappy thought or feeling we hold dear within our heart and head was represented by a large pebble stowed safely away in a precious imaginary rucksack we carried with us everywhere we went. I guess it would be quite full! It stands to reason you would soon get tired and become totally exhausted with carrying around such a heavy weight on your back. The sensible move would be to remove the rucksack from your back, reducing the weight by discarding the contents, carefully removing the pebbles one by one from the rucksack and throwing them away.

You will by now be very aware of the distance travelled on your life's journey. The challenges and achievements met and mastered, the achievable goals and targets ahead, immeasurably linked with raw insight and disquiet into the realisation how much heavy baggage you have unwittingly accumulated on your journey. As the distance traversed has been so great, it now makes perfect sense to actually assess how much baggage you really are carrying in your imaginary rucksack.

Once recognised, honesty and courage will be the requirement to make yet another decision. Do you really want to carry your weighty baggage with you always? Do you really have the confidence and faith to permanently get rid of your heavy load? If "courage" and "conviction" are your passwords and you willingly choose to change your life by taking this course of action, your immense reward will be an empowered enlightened YOU. You will consciously feel uplifted in your heart and head, aware of a lightness of spirit you had not noticed before.

You need to ask yourself yet another very important question. Are you truly happy with the ingrained habits of a lifetime, feeling always duty-bound to others, encumbering yourself with unhappy painful and emotional imprints of the past?

Now trust and allow the unseen forces of God to awaken the senses within, to heal the passage of time, erasing painful hurts, dispelling shadows of inadequacy, removing inhibited confidence, harbouring guilt and disillusion. Have courage; display personal bravery by now moving the chess pieces of life into the right position for you to awaken a new beginning, a new chapter of life. Allow events to unfold, as designated. Be patient and go with the flow of life. From this point on, do not push or try to manipulate people or events. Allow your life to open up as it is supposed to as the universal blueprint dictates. Remember that God, the angelic realms, our guides and helpers know what is the best and right path. Just trust that all will be well.

DISCARDING UNWANTED BAGGAGE

This exercise, although simplistic, may take time, so be patient

Now is the perfect time to quietly admit to yourself the deluge of illusory negative imprints you have been nurturing all these years. It is an opportunity to recall painful memories, images you now recognise as hindering your ability to forge ahead, preventing you from recognising your true potential, blocking an ability to recognise new opportunities when they arose.

Look past the invisible armadillo shell you have erected around your being. Acknowledge the need to let go. Recognise with painful honesty past regrets, disappointments and negative reactions that still continue to cast a shadow over your life. Have the courage to dig deep within, bringing to the surface destructive, hurtful baggage you would like to obliterate if you could.

I am sure you would not harbour clutter or rubbish in a home or place of work you are proud of, so why hold on tight to hurtful words, images and disappointments? Take courage in both hands. Discard your unwanted baggage. Clear the path ahead. Take a big leap forward.

To prepare yourself for this undertaking, when you feel the time is right, seek a quiet time. Go somewhere you can be still and peaceful, ensuring that you are not disturbed by unexpected interruptions or the intrusion of beloved pets or telephones. With courage in both hands, now is the time to bring to the surface painful innermost thoughts, negative emotions and feelings you wish you could destroy and to discard forever. Initially, you may find this contemplation extremely difficult to grasp as you have unwittingly, secretly and unknowingly been harbouring powerful, controlling and obstructive imprints for years. A lifetime's habit has had an unrivalled impression on your life, unintentionally becoming comfortable and familiar. You may ask yourself a little fearfully what will fill the void and replace this weight of negativity. The replacement will be a consciousness of self-belief and clarity.

The importance of this exercise is to do it at your own pace when you feel ready. You may decide "This is the day – my new beginning," then talk yourself out of the process. Be reassured you have so much strength and tenacity you will proceed when the timing is right. Remember, you have embarked on an unfamiliar journey. This proposed action is new and a little scary.

You will by now be exploring many avenues of life from your earliest memories to this point in time. This will involve reliving and resurrecting feelings you may have felt you had buried deep within your depths, completely unaware until today how these hurts have reflected in your attitude to life, your perception of yourself and others, your ability to truly show and give love, and equally as important to love and honour your very being.

When you feel ready, equip yourself with a pen or pencil, paper or notepad and seek your selected quiet room where you will not be disturbed by noise. In reality, probably the best time is when you can take advantage of the quiet of an empty home, with space completely to yourself. Set aside a block of quiet quality time for your intended endeavour. Relax and be comfortable. Be patient. Allow sufficient time for you to quietly go within and to be still.

After a short while, you will feel relaxed. Your mind will cease to race and will be still. When you sense a change of vibration, a gentle peace within and surrounding you, ask your guides to draw close to help you, to ensure free flow of energy to encircle you and to shower you with love and light while enveloping you with a cloak of protection. Ask for their strength, guidance and courage for what is about to take place. Breathe deeply until a rhythmic breathing pattern has been established.

When you feel totally at peace and sense the time is right, pick up a piece of paper folding it in half lengthways, so in effect you have two halves. Now place the folded piece of paper in front of you. With the fold on the right hand side of you, write the heading "Unwanted Baggage." With focus, intent and raw honesty, write down a phrase or word only you understand, plus the name or names of people, situations or events you feel have had a negative affect on your life, leaving a scar on your psyche. Be extremely patient and take your time when writing this list as it is crucial and very, very important. If you feel you need to use more than one piece of paper that is fine. Remember that this process is special and precious. Possibly for the first time in your life, you are focussing on YOU, your innermost thoughts and feelings.

You will feel emotional as you write, recalling a kaleidoscope of images. Tears may trickle down your cheeks. You may sob with real pain and some released relief, perhaps for the first time in your life admitting to yourself the circumstance, comment, action or event that has overshadowed your life, scoring a deep mark in your psyche. This process takes tremendous courage, producing deep-seated emotions and hard fought back tears, which, believe me, are wonderful healing tears.

While still in a state of emotional enfoldment, turn over the piece of paper, with the fold now on your left side. Write the heading "Unspoken List." With emotions still bubbling, body aching, eyes and cheeks wet with tears, write a list of your hopes and dreams. Write from the heart, again one or two words, or as many as you wish, to remind you of your wishes and desires for the future, and where you really want to be in your life. What pathway do you visualise for yourself? Write your hopes and dreams, your aspirations, your childhood inspirations. Write the opportunities you would like to see manifest and the course of action you would like to take if given the opportunity. Pen challenges you know you can master given the right circumstances. In essence, write your "Wish List."

When you have finished writing, turn the paper back to the list headed "Unwanted Baggage" and slowly read through the list. Sit quietly for a few moments. Ask yourself if you have forgotten to add anything. If so, add it to the list. This is a very emotive list, your list, one for your eyes only.

Now you are ready to release, for always, your heavy imaginary rucksack brimming with unhappy negative contents.

Relax. Close your eyes. Still your mind.

Visualise you have just landed at a busy international airport. There's hustle and bustle everywhere. Everyone appears very busy, with queues of passengers waiting to book in and people milling around waiting to greet travellers off the aircraft. There appears to be order despite the apparent chaos.

The airport is heaving with hundreds of people of all nationalities tending suitcases, bags, children and buggies, either patiently waiting or hurrying, all focussing on their purpose ahead.

Flickering information screens, drifting aroma of fresh ground coffee and newly-baked rolls, bombardment of numerous messages over the airport Tannoy public address system, baggage collection points and lumbering luggage trolleys colour the mood of the arrival and departure lounges. Airport staff are immaculately turned out in their pristine uniforms, busy and attentive as usual. The airport is a hive of activity!

You are returning from an unexpected short holiday away in the sunshine, a rest from work and home. You feel refreshed, your mind and body benefiting greatly from the wonderful opportunity to stop and switch off, a break you really enjoyed. You feel invigorated, relaxed and uplifted, with hope in your heart for a new beginning, a new chapter. All the pressures, cares and woes of everyday life seem to be a million miles away.

You stroll through passport control, "Duty Frees" purchased on the aircraft safe in your hand luggage. You are brought back to reality with a bump when you come face to face with the frenetic energy of the populous rushing to and fro. Slowly and reluctantly, you descend into reality, aware that the upbeat feeling of calm and upliftment within is beginning to recede.

You reach the airport carousel, with travellers from numerous flights patiently waiting to identify their luggage to continue their onward journey. You stop and wait, in a mesmerised state, lost in a moment of time, staring ahead, a glazed look in your eyes.

You gradually become aware of a stranger standing to the right of you, smiling. The stranger's presence felt strangely welcoming and pleasant. You do not speak. You do not question his purpose for being there. He asks, as if by telepathic means,

"How did you feel when you were away?"
*"Do you the feel the break from routine and monotonous pressure
        of life was beneficial?"*
" How do you feel after your break?"
*"Are you really looking forward to picking up the threads of your
        life when you return home, rejoining the place of your work?"*
"Did you make any major decisions when you were away?"
*"In hindsight, are there any changes you would like to make to your
        life if circumstances were different?"*
"Do you feel you will miss the people you met while you were away?"
*"Did you achieve all you planned to do while away? Do you have
        any regrets?"*
*"Is there anything you brought back with you from your break away
        which you feel on reflection has very little benefit or purpose?"*

The unspoken questions resonate against the noisy backdrop of the frenetic airport, being fired in quick succession, one after another, then for no explicable reason, there was silence...

"I wonder – is there anything you no longer need in life which you would care to leave here and now in this busy airport terminal before you continue your onward journey if that was possible?"

You reluctantly break free from your stupor, suddenly becoming aware that your luggage has been set down neatly beside you: a baggage handler has identified it as yours. You realise you are still in a soporific state. Looking around, you realise with utter amazement you seem to be alone; the other passengers have collected their luggage and are a distance away.

The stranger again asks the question, "Is there any baggage you would like to throw away, to permanently leave behind before you travel home?"

It is at this moment you realise you hold in your hand the list you previously wrote through tears of pain and grief – the list of words, events and circumstances creating a wall of unwelcome blockages, creating distance from loved ones, fuelling heartache, anger and discord.

In a split second awakening, you realise you have been given a once in a lifetime chance to let go, to throw away years and years of accumulated baggage you have been guarding so tight.

The stranger interjects – "It is your choice, your decision!"

In that instant, you realise this is the opportunity you have been waiting, praying and secretly hoping for. You instinctively know you have the stranger's support, sensing he cares and has your interest at heart. You realise in that moment you are being given a wonderful opening to make big sweeping life changes.

You struggle with emotions, questioning yourself, trying to ascertain whether you still possess the tenacity and courage to throw away forever the many painful hurts and negativity lodged deep in your heart and head.

The stranger asks again, "Do you really wish to let go of your unwanted baggage? If so, have you the courage to place your imaginary rucksack, complete with all unwanted baggage, on the moving carousel in front of you? Be alert to the fact that once you have made this emotive gesture, the carousel will slowly revolve, gradually moving away out of sight with all your discarded baggage, never, ever to be seen or retrieved by you again. Make your decision; place with purpose and intent your baggage on the carousel. Now watch your baggage slowly move away from you until completely out of sight."

You grasp the chance with both hands, placing the rucksack purposefully on the carousel. Transfixed, you watch the carousel steadily moving out of your line of vision. After watching the carousel revolve, you look around; the stranger is still close by, smiling, now emitting a magnificent aura of rainbow colours. You become enveloped in a wonderful feeling of peace and warmth. You become aware you are encircled with love and light, a power source surging through your energy centres. You look down at the piece of paper still clutched firmly in your hand.

You notice glancing down at the "Unwanted Baggage" list, so painstakingly written. The paper is blank, with every single word and mark erased! You turn the folded piece of paper over, seeking any changes to the list you had written under the heading "Unspoken List." It was under this heading you wrote your wish list of hopes and dreams, places to visit and people to see. You notice that the heading has changed, being replaced with the word "Future."

With a turn of the head, your eyes meet the stranger's eyes, locked in a wealth of compassion, love and deep understanding. In that moment, his energy, wisdom and image is captured in your imagination. You are truly blessed; you have come face to face with your guide. Your higher self is free. In that instant you accept, although you may not always see him with your mind's eye, that he is with you always. THANK YOU MY GUIDE.

Looking at the list again, awareness dawns that you can write and live your own future. You realise in that instant everywhere looks vibrant and radiant. You are truly alive, sensing your newly found power. You have miraculously tapped into an inner source of truth and energy. You know everything you desire is not as unachievable as it seems. You have the power to create all you need.

You now have the self-belief to realise you have the power to change or heal anything in your life you wish to change. With inbuilt wisdom and knowledge, you can tap into this power source at any time. You are truly free of dogma, restrictions and limitations of the past. *You are free.*

Your have travelled a long way on your journey. You have been empowered and enlightened. In the fullness of time, you will come to recognise the importance of clearing your path.

During the journey of discovery, many students berate themselves, creating pain and heartache, especially when they do not heed the guidance of the Higher Realms. Be of stout heart, for this day you have recognised a great truth. Your pathway ahead is now defined. You cannot turn back; there will be no regrets. Life is for living.

Rope

Like a rope, tightly bound
We enter the world, safe and sound
A silver thread from there to here
Always attached whether you be dark or fair

Three equal strands this rope does have
Physical, spiritual, emotional to find a path
That is just right for every single soul
Gaining in strength and character to reach your goal

Our physical needs are simply said
Fresh air, replenishing sleep and daily bread
Emotionally we need to love and care
Knowing there is someone always there

The spiritual side is the finest
Needs nourishment of the very best
To feel complete and true to oneself
Sometimes thinking of others before thyself

One cannot share what you cannot feel
For life is an on-going intricate wheel
A mind not at ease leads to disease
So seek contentment, live with ease

To live, enjoy each new day
Whether busy at work or just at play
Happiness is purely a state of mind
To enrich living life's lessons of every kind

So be happy, bright and true
For family, friends and especially you
For we are all very special in our way
Walking our chosen path, proud and gay

The strands must always remain tight
Protecting from the wrongs and right
Helping us to forge a path so strong
We will always feel safe, knowing we belong.

Chapter 13
The Awakening

*To emerge or arouse from a sleep state; to become aware and alert; to consciously remember memories; to be "**awake**."*

Over centuries, great wisdom has been immersed in chants and writings to inspire, reassure, delivering comfort and upliftment, unknowingly supporting mankind's allotted passage of time on this earth plane. Before we dispense with our mortal frame, I wonder how many really reflect back on their life's journey so far with delight and recognition of achievements gained by hard work and effort. How many recognise the many challenges accomplished despite the odds with a sense of justified pride and completion, silently acknowledging strong determination, the will and sense of purpose that enabled them to fulfil their destiny? They know they made it; they achieved their impossible dream.

Over the years, I have spent many hours with people who live with regret, a longing to relive their lives, tinged with the comment "In hindsight, if things had been different..." How often I have listened to the sighs of despondency – "I wish I had worked harder at school" or "I wish I had." To listen and empathise with an unhappy sitter draws me closer to them, especially when a torrid of negative emotions of resentment, jealously and past irrational behaviour are released to the surface, initially dominating the reason the person has come. The true essence of a reading often brings to the surface doubts and fears of the past, reliving a lost passage of time and opportunities, with these remorseful words often being said – "I wish I had. If I come to this earth plane again, I will achieve. I will succeed."

How many of you reading these words can truthfully say you are where you want to be in life? Are you at peace with yourself? Are you in an environment where you are encouraged to achieve your full potential? If hand on heart you can say "Yes!" warm congratulations are yours and richly deserved. You need then to ask yourself two other points – "Why?" and "How?" What sets you apart from the crowd? What makes you different from others? Why do you feel you have achieved where others have seemingly failed?

As a spark of the divine, we are delivered into this world enveloped in a naked coat, exhibiting the physical frame we chose before we agreed to spend time on Mother Earth. We depart this world the same way. Material acquisitions gained over a lifetime's endeavour are simply that, earthly trappings that serve no spiritual purpose and of no real consequence on our onward journey. However, we do leave behind a valuable impression of our existence, an imprint of our life-span on this earth. The depth and size of the imprint is dependent on the life we led.

As we grow in stature and maturity, our perception, achievements and priorities change in line with the seasons and the distinct chapters of our life. Our bodies too take on the mantle of the seasons, from the spring and summer of our lives moving towards the autumn and winter of our life, when we can, depending on our perception, feel a little vulnerable, tending to mull over the highs and lows of life's journey on earth. This is a personal, private, quiet time to ponder on the legacy we will eventually leave behind. Nothing lasts forever; all manner of life evolves in the fullness of time. The winter of our lives should be a joyous time of celebration, to bathe in the glory of past achievements, to recapture happy memories, to relive challenges and endeavours with pride and relief, silently evaluating our chosen pathway.

The true purpose and destiny for our life-span on Mother Earth is known only to each individual soul. We journey to this earth plane to learn lessons – lessons we chose to agree and accept before we are born. I also believe we choose our potential talents and pathway, being fully equipped with all the skills necessary to help us achieve our ultimate challenges and fulfilment should we decide to walk that path.

We should acknowledge that all pre-agreed challenges and potential for a successful pathway are hidden deep within our consciousness. The doorway to knowledge and insight is easily located when true thirst for knowledge and quest for answers is sincere and profound. We are also blessed with the gift of free will, an ability to make our own decisions and choices, to furrow our own path. Sometimes this follows an insistent inspirational inner insight pointing the way to a route we know we must follow, even though we may have no idea where it is leading.

The emergence of insight and wisdom tends to dawn only after living through many chapters of our lives. We all have lessons to learn. Many spend most of their waking days amassing great wealth. Sadly, more often than not, this is at the expense of family relationships in a compulsion to gather more and more and more, in the process losing sight of the real meaning of life – the gift of life itself.

We are all sometimes too busy to notice the wonderful intricate world in which we live, to take a sharp intake of breath when marvelling at the creation and enrichment of life in its many forms. To ponder at the many as yet unsolved mysteries of the oceans' depths. To respect the sometimes devastating impact unrelenting changeable weather systems have on landmasses and oceans. To accept how insignificant we really are in the grand scheme of life in relation to the solar system and beyond. We indulge with delight and romanticise the magic of moonbeams whilst accepting the moon's powerful effect on Mother Earth, although we still do not fully comprehend its full force and affect on tidal forces and oceans' currents, its awesome power and mystery still yet to be understood by mere mortal man.

We take for granted the diverse seasonal cycles of planet earth and bitterly complain when they appear out of sync. We contemplate with respect the awesome force, strength, power and beautiful regeneration of Mother Nature. From time to time, we stop to reflect on the sheer miracle of life, its essence and its energy in all its many forms.

Great wealth and the burden it carries can be cold comfort when looking back at a path trodden so far when the realisation dawns, in horror, that past choices and motives have been unbalanced. A simple unexpected catalyst awakens a conscious awareness that people really do matter. Sometimes, you can seem to have everything in a material sense yet in essence nothing of true value.

Material possessions can be destroyed and removed in a trice. One valued commodity no amount of money can buy is the devotion, love and companionship of life-long friends and family. It has been known that the burden of accumulating great wealth and status can cause great anxiety and concern towards the end of a life. The enormous strain and responsibility of deciding the best and right way to distribute such vast amassed wealth weighs heavily, the billionaire inwardly knowing and reluctantly accepting that others will never, ever understand the sacrifice and heartache endured in the push to succeed. When great wealth is distributed willingly, joy can also be short-lived, especially if choices are made late in life, leaving little time to witness the change and happiness monetary gifts can create. The sacrifice and energy is seemingly lost in the fullness of time. I believe the greatest legacy you can leave anyone is: "***Remember me for loving you***".

We live in a technological age, a material age, when we are seemingly judged on how we dress and live. Paper money and coins of the realm are the recognised currency for exchange of goods or services in today's world. Gone are the days when we exchanged corn, livestock and man's labour as a means for meeting our needs. We need to earn enough for our essential needs, food, shelter and warmth while endeavouring to maintain balance in all areas of our lives.

Time is precious; the greatest gift you can give anyone is your time.

Giving a little time willingly, a small part of you, unleashes a wonderful sense of feeling good, a sprinkling of joy. It may simply be a smile, an exchange of kind words, a helping hand to a friend or neighbour, or just the offer of support to a stranger in need. Remember that a smile is repaid immediately with another smile. It is infectious – try it some time!

We sadly question and deliberate why we live in these troubled, turbulent times, searching for the answer to where humanity is heading. We therefore must also acknowledge that some people are born achievers with vision, focus and a determination to succeed. Others seemingly appear to struggle, striving and juggling time, people and situations in a never-ending search for a better future.

Some work slowly and perseveringly towards fulfilling their perceived purpose. Others, if they are truly honest with themselves, just exist like flotsam floating on the sea, unsure of how to change direction, how to really live their life or how to find their true pathway. They also wonder how to find inner peace and contentment.

Living life to the full whilst accepting with raw honestly the person we truly are, acknowledging strengths, weaknesses, little foibles, doubts and fears, is tough and a little scary. We are at our most content when giving of our best, willingly using our natural gifts and talents. Being the kind of person we truly believe we are is not simple or easy, but this is why we chose to live on this earth plane at this point in time. If we were perfect, there would be no earthly reason for us to be here at all.

Despite outward appearances, I believe we choose to return to this earth plane, consenting to many agreed challenges prior to our birth and sanctioning the goals we agreed to face. One very important choice is our parentage, the culture and circumstances we are born into, our choice of parents being the strongest and finest foundation stone for the springboard of lessons and challenges we chose to master. Our choice and reasoning for our existence is hidden deep within our consciousness. We need to graciously thank our parents for the role they played and the valuable lessons learned.

The prior agreement of choosing our parents is the key foundation stone for our success, beautifully equipping us for the key lessons we agreed and chose to master. Once a challenge is conquered, the lesson moves, remains in the past and is never presented again. We need to admit that we all have personal innermost challenges to overcome, our choice of environment, culture, creed, privilege or lack of it being a ledge of the mountain range we chose to climb.

Our private innermost world may be full of thoughts, feelings, anxieties, concerns, doubts and fears which we do not fully understand. We may question why we seem to find ourselves in a particular situation. Why does this happen? What is life all about? We sense unseen pressure building around us. We admit to ourselves we are not always comfortable with the way we handle stressful situations, aware unwelcome pressure harbours many mountainous thoughts and feelings. We can become extremely anxious when faced with the chance of verbalising or expressing deep thoughts and feelings for fear of admitting vulnerability.

I believe there is a simple formula for tapping into your true potential, setting anxiety to one side while releasing insight and answers you have deep within your very being, constantly generating a crystal clear solution to the numerous challenges that beset you on your life's journey. Utilising with complete trust the wealth of wisdom, knowledge and confidence within enables you to be the person you truly are, heralding sight of your chosen pathway. This empowers you to live your life and reach your full potential while maintaining essential balance.

One footstep onto the pathway is the first step to a new beginning. Your chosen journey may not always be smooth. If it were, lessons would not be mastered. However, you will soon find during your journey that big boulders miraculously turn into pebbles and swollen rivers into streams.

$$\textbf{Acceptance} \rightarrow \textbf{Belief} \rightarrow \textbf{Focus} \rightarrow \textbf{Trust}$$
$$= \textbf{Empowerment \& Completion}$$

This tried and tested formula works. Do not doubt it!

To step on the first rung of any ladder takes thought, will and intent to make that move. The acceptance and determination to believe you can take this first step is probably the most difficult step you will take. The rest is comparatively easy, moving upwards one step at a time, knowing you will reach the top rung.

ACCEPTANCE

We may not truly understand why we feel as we do sometimes and why occasionally we feel as if we do not belong. We need to accept our environment and roots as being a huge part of us - our birthright. Yet we may still question from time to time "Why me?" feeling slightly troubled and awkward moving through this thought process.

A huge part of changing direction, of moving forward, of questioning, is a natural process. You may not be aware, but in fact you are challenging yourself. WHY? You are now allowing yourself to be in touch with your inner self on a different level, drawing closer to the inner you, your inner core, your higher self, empowering you to delve further to uncover concealed impressions and feelings, accepting, perhaps for the first time, hidden qualities. An awakening occurs of why these powerful thoughts and visions have eluded you before now. We accept and acknowledge nurturing yet sometimes find it difficult to accept and understand some situations, especially if we sense we do not quite fit into the pattern shape seemingly laid out for us.

During this period of awakening, the timescale determined by yourself, the awareness of your inner wisdom increases. We need to learn to listen to the inner voice within and to acknowledge the validity of our thoughts, visions and dreams. Remember that you have all the answers within; you just need to trust an unseen guardian to help you find the key to reveal the wealth of gifts, talents and energies concealed deep within. Humbly and willingly accept that you are unique. Acknowledge with joy changes in your thoughts and feelings. Listen and act without any further delay.

You will more than likely go through a life review at this stage trying to unravel a puzzle. Be gentle with yourself and others at this time while aiming to change anything in your life you feel is unbalanced. Take courage in both hands: allow an unfolding to occur to reveal who you truly are. With excitement and trust accept the pathway you are drawn to.

We need to accept and believe in ourselves, to cast aside all negativity, doubts and fear to instinctively know we can achieve and climb the highest mountain. To acknowledge and know if our desire and motivation is right that the summit is already within reach. We will then be able to tap into a wealth of insight, wisdom and courage to face the mountain and start that climb. Sometimes it takes sheer courage and human endeavour to break out of the mould we find ourselves in, to believe everything is possible, the degree of strength and determination dependent on the flame of desire and intent.

We readily accept we are not all destined to be rocket scientists, but we all have a purpose and destiny to fulfil. Believe that you chose your destiny prior to birth, safely delivered to Mother Earth fully equipped for the challenges you agreed to overcome and master. This is why our parents' foundation stone is so important.

We live in a fast-moving media age, a technological age, our mindset sometimes seeming to be pre-programmed to world events. Sometimes we find great difficulty in comprehending real-life events unfolding before our eyes. We have seemingly become blasé to watching a journalist's televised broadcast from a fragmented war-torn land. The ongoing constant stream of information from all media sources sometimes confuses fact from fiction. This perpetual invasion distorts the clear distinction between the latest blockbuster movie, recreating a writer's fantasy of the same ilk and live coverage of actual human tragic events.

Our minds are bombarded ferociously with information from the time we open our eyes to the time we go to bed. We are given little respite from the constant pressure of news coverage on radio, television, tabloids and broadsheets. We are surrounded by the constant stress and noise of the 21st century. We need to be respectful of the value of allowing ourselves to enjoy quality "Me" time, for peace and quiet is essential to find our inner self. Time is so precious; we need sometimes to consciously turn our backs on the constant barrage of information, seemingly locked in negativity. To consciously allow quality precious "ME" time to take place, to find an opportunity to be quiet and aware of the higher self.

You need to trust guidance from within. Remember that only you truly understands "YOU." No one really knows or understands your hopes, dreams and desires deep within. By allowing yourself vital quality time, you can go within, be in touch with your inner core of peace and become acquainted with your essence, allowing time and space to be in touch with your higher self. Recognise that higher energies are ready and waiting to guide your first step on the ladder of your chosen pathway. We are all unique, our pathway being chosen before we come to this earth plane to experience, to learn, to grow and to expand our horizons. The immensity of the pathway is not paramount. What is important is the personal endeavour and effort expended in reaching your goal.

Great writers, they say, are born. That is true, but each one of you, I know, would be able to pen a story, an experience that touched you deeply. The most acclaimed writers write about what they know, what they feel, how love and hate have impacted on their lives. They write as it is, complete with ugly embellishments, the words being honest and true. You need to do the same; you owe it to yourself to be the person you truly are. Recognise and acknowledge when you are on the wrong path. Have the courage to change direction if that feels right. Learn to listen to the still, small voice inside – your higher self.

Listen to the still voice inside

– "your higher self" –

It will never let you down

Imagine there is a little light switch inside you which, when turned on, will awaken your true potential. Have the courage to flick the switch. Wait and see what happens! You are in control of your pathway. You will not let yourself down. Your higher self will not let you down, so you have nothing to fear.

BELIEF

Our belief system is coloured by our upbringing, our environment, our formative years and to a greater extent is dictated by our parents' beliefs and background. It unravels the mystery of our destiny and purpose, which sometimes remains dormant until we reach our teens. It is about this time that hormones come into play and we feel rebellious, feeling a need to assert ourselves when in reality we are unknowingly questioning the scenario we find ourselves in. We feel the need to react to decisions dictated by others, sensing a need to be ourselves, reacting to a calling from our inner being.

This process can be as easy or as difficult as we choose to make it. Gauging parental patterns can be illuminating, sometimes straddling the line of acceptance of who we truly are while appeasing the dreams our parents have for us. Unspoken high expectations can be stressful and difficult. Eventually, we break free, finding the courage to believe in our future, our pathway, our choice, finding our true self.

We need to nurture confidence and believe in our abilities. To master natural gifts and talents, no matter how difficult. To succumb to the will to succeed, to accept setbacks not failure while realising sometimes we need to take one step back in order to move forward three. As children, we strive for adulthood and choice, but once reached, we question and doubt what life is all about. I am urging you to believe in yourself, your abilities and to acknowledge that you can achieve anything and everything you set your heart and mind on.

You can with quiet confidence put your foot on the second rung of the ladder. You can achieve the impossible dream; you just need to believe in yourself and to listen to your small voice within. Remember that your higher self will never let you down. Keep a journal and log your chosen pathway. Map the necessary stages, but do not be impatient. Allow stepping-stones on your pathway to be revealed at the right time. Your still, small voice will prompt you and keep you on the right pathway, so learn to listen, believe and accept.

FOCUS

The content of conversations with people who already walk a spiritual path sincerely refer to "love and light." These are words with an impact. One of the many definitions of "focus" is the convergence of light or soundwaves, a point at which they converge. By now, you will believe in the power of love and light, the energy of the words "acceptance," "belief" and "focus" creating a balanced harmony.

We need to focus in order to achieve; if our concentration wavers, the magic of the moment is gone. We need to accept the art of being able to focus, acknowledging auric energy revealing us as a joyous work of art. It is impossible for a sense of achievement and fulfilment to be measured by others. Great scientists and scholars did not achieve their fame by being disorientated, disorganised or lazy. Their channelled energy was driven by the focussed desire to achieve and to prove to themselves they could.

In this materialistic world in which we live, I often hear the phase "She is lucky!" What the onlooker sees is the fruits of the labour. They do not see or choose to see the dedication, energy, belief and focus of the achievement. They choose only to see the end result.

So much has been achieved by so many during the last century. Tremendous progress has been made in medicine. Many are still fiercely determined and dedicated in the pursuit of discovering cost-effective and proactive ways of improving the health and quality of life for others. They devise ingenuous processes to improve and heal horrific injuries caused through accidents and war. They soldier on, demonstrating unwavering dedication, perseverance and focus, ignoring many setbacks.

Many entrepreneurs and successful businessmen take calculated risks, alongside trusting a vision and belief in their endeavours. Once reached, their initial horizon of wealth may appear to be an empty victory, with the thought "Where do I go from here?" Many achieve joy and contentment by using their knowledge and wealth to help others, humanity benefiting from the wealth of experience gained on their journey of success.

In their obsession to achieve, some unknowingly tread the path of destiny, using their acquired power and wealth to ease the suffering of humanity, silently joyous in being able to make a big difference to this world. Instead of congratulating the risk takers' success, some onlookers seem too quick to proffer negative comments by criticism, judging motivation and seeking an unfound hidden agenda. They fail once again to acknowledge with admiration the time, dedication and tireless energy expended in order to expand their horizons to achieve their chosen goal. Some begrudge other peoples' success, which is hurtful and negative. Use your energy wisely; use it to create your own success.

TRUST

By now, you will be aware of your small voice within (some call it intuition). You need to listen with heartening delight to each snippet of wisdom and information. Respond willingly and act when required. It is a huge part of the very essence of who you are. It will never, ever let you down.

Rejection and disappointment affect us all at some time or another, to a greater or lesser degree. It may come through the guise of a friend, a work colleague, family or simply feeling disappointed in oneself, perhaps doubting the ability to face a particular situation or rising to a specific challenge. The emotion and feeling of being let down, in whatever form, leaves an ache of emptiness with expectations crushed, uncovering resentment and hurt. This is the negativity of experiencing disappointment and rejection.

The positive is renewed energy, acknowledging and seeing the situation or event in its true light. We realise that an experience served only to heighten awareness of people and life's challenges, strengthening a resolve to move forward. The realisation gradually wakes that although emotionally dispiriting, the disappointment has gently pushed you onto a new direction.

We all have free will in the decisions we make. We also discover in the fullness of time whether our choice has been wise or foolish. Remember, there is always a flip side to every negative situation. In the fullness of time, positive blessings can always be discovered.

When we eventually reach a point of admitting to ourselves that our judgement was a little awry or a wrong decision was made, an opportunity for change soon follows to restore the status quo. So from now on listen to your higher self before you embark on a life-changing decision. I cannot reiterate too strongly the joy, upliftment and strength you will discover in trusting your still, small voice. By trusting and listening, you will become whom you choose to be.

Life is all about enjoying the journey, complete with its ups and downs. Take in and enjoy the scenery on the way. See the whole picture. Trust and listen to your inner voice for it will always guide you. Eventually, your faith and trust in your higher self will encourage you to be receptive to the vibrant spiritual energies surrounding you, always ready and willing to accompany you on your onward journey. The more you trust, the easier your life will become. You will inevitably become stronger, unknowingly blending with vibrations of the Higher Realms, who will guide, teach and reassure you.

EMPOWERMENT / COMPLETION

There is only one true enemy to fulfilling your true potential and finding the sparkle that belongs only to you – and that is "fear." Fear of the unknown pathway ahead.

Unfortunately, the essence of fear is an uncomfortable feeling of apprehension, a sensation of alarm fuelling a deep-seated anxiety within the solar plexus, heightened by insecurities, created or instilled into us by others. The fear of losing someone we love; the fear of not meeting other people's expectations of us; the fear of failing; the fear of being rejected; the fear of being regarded as "the fool." The list is endless! Does it sound familiar?

I spend time with many young people whose fears are irrational yet nevertheless very real to them, encompassing unhappy deep-seated thoughts and feelings. Time spent with them is invaluable in helping them understand themselves. In hindsight, some of my choices in life, especially during my formative years, would have been very different if I had had the opportunity of spending time with someone willing to impart wisdom and spiritual truths. I now realise how easy it would have been for them to dispel my doubts and fears at that time, which I now accept with grace was all part of my learning curve for me to experience the incredible range of highs and lows life brings. This first-hand knowledge now enables me to help others. I firmly believe it is nigh impossible to imagine how another feels unless you have experienced their pain.

In later years, I was very privileged and blessed to spend time with a very special spiritual man, someone from another culture. I talked and he listened. He dissolved my inner pain, dissipated my doubts and fears, empowering me to be who I am this day. I asked if he knew of a formula, a magic tool, I could share with others to help them eradicate deep ingrained fears they know block their progress. I share this very special formula with you now.

It really is quite simplistic and very easy to understand. Believe me: as you use this formula, any deep hurt and pain will dissipate. Emptiness will be replaced with a euphoria of strength, courage and self-belief, reconfirming that you are unique and special in every way, reinforcing a burnished ambition to achieve your heart's desire. You will acknowledge hidden gifts and qualities within; you will reach out with confidence and be who you truly are.

You will suddenly be aware of balance creeping into every area of your life, revealing an energy encouraging you to be YOU. You will not doubt. You will face life with diligence and raw honesty. Your fears will be seen for what they really are. Anxieties no longer have any power. In essence, you will become empowered to be the unique person you are. You will no longer question your future or your onward journey: you will focus with a fierce determination to face the mountain range head on, allowing your destiny to unfold before you, enabling you to shine and be the special person you truly are. You will find renewed energy, desire and the iron will to reach for the stars. You will recognise problems as merely challenging stepping-stones to be overcome. You will conquer the doubting fearful enemy within.

Remember the following:

F = Fear	transform to	F-Faith
O = Own Way	transform to	O-Obedience
E = Emptiness	transform to	E-Empowerment

Fear – of the future, of discovering your potential, who you truly are!	→	**Faith** – in the magnificent spark of divine – that is YOU!
Own Way – ignoring inner wisdom and truth, resulting in struggles!	→	**Obedience** – to listen and act on inspired guidance from within!
Emptiness – feeling incomplete, searching for the missing something!	→	**Empower** – to release your potential, setting your higher self-free to follow your destiny!

A wonderful formula to master – the old definition of FOE is now an outdated memory.

You are now empowered to tread on the first step of your new pathway. Congratulations! ENJOY THE EXPERIENCE.

Exercise – The Awakening
Note challenging issues. Why do you question? Note what has changed in your life.

Note subtle changes in your perception, your focus and your need to make changes. When did your empowerment begin?

_ _

_ _

_ _

_ _

_ _

_ _

_ _

_ _

_ _

_ _

_ _

_ _

_ _

_ _

_ _

_ _

_ _

_ _

Trust

Shed not a tear for I am here
Have no fear for I am always near
To share the pain and give relief
So please no sad heart full of grief

Your earth is a truly wondrous place
Colours of every hue to grace
The animals, trees, birds and bees
Sky, earth, mountain range and seas

Every day brings something new
Every minute offers a changing view
Nothing ever stays the same
Except God, who always takes the blame

The blame when things don't work out right
And we lay awake in the still of night
To relieve the hurt and guilt we feel
For times past, like a spinning wheel.

Enjoy the brightness of each new day
Shed not a tear, just pray and pray
Knowing an answer will be given
Especially for you direct from heaven

For heaven registers every single thought
Every desire and wish that's sought
Is answered in a special way
Except we are not given the time or day

So know there is a reason why
Blessings are sent from on high
Know a special person you will always be
To your family, friends and especially me

So take courage in both hands
As healing love travels across the land
To uplift, holding you very tight
Keeping you safe with God from morn to night

Chapter 14
Awareness

Unknowingly, we are all on a journey of discovery, questioning from time to time, "Where we are heading? What is our purpose?" Many have achieved so much, measuring success by the acquisition of material trappings. Many have clear career objectives, leading to rapid promotional advantageous circumstances, yearning to reach the key status of best high-flyer in the workplace.

Some desire to take advantage of the numerous opportunities to travel, exploring other countries, absorbing their lifestyle and cogitating on beliefs and cultures of other nations. To a certain extent this determines their own pathway in life yet in raw honesty how many are truly really happy and content with who they are, their acquired status in life, their perception of life, and are really and truly satisfied with the pathway they walk at this moment in time?

The media, although intrusive at times, has opened our eyes and hearts to a seemingly simplistic life led by many tribal groups who have, up to now, escaped the pressures of modern civilisation yet appear to have discovered the secret of "inner peace," our terminology for Shangri-La. Recent televised reality programmes have given some fortunate Westerners a unique opportunity of stepping out of their comfort zone to live and participate in a typical tribal environment. Although an initial shock to the system, being shielded from the frenetic whirlpool of life allowed them to take time out, to reflect, observe, to be awakened to the importance of being unencumbered, perhaps for the first time highlighting where their priorities lie.

Tribal peoples not tainted by the pressured modern world remain content and cushioned in their hierarchy and family groups, happy living in an environment that meets all their simple requirements of the day. They may be regarded as illiterate and lacking in comparison to the academic educated West and East. However, we can learn much from their depth of care and respect for their environment and each other. Their unpretentious lifestyle, deep within a seemingly impenetrable jungle, has a respected and uncomplicated order that works. In simple terms, they consider one another's needs. They respect the existence of wildlife and the animal kingdom, working with nature rather than against it. Their beliefs and way of life are passed down through the generations, obliviously ignorant of any other lifestyle or circumstance.

Modern-day inveterate travellers who visit these little known groups of humanity readily admit to being featherbedded by our twenty-first century society. Though the visit may be short, the experience leaves an indelible emotional imprint of sheer disbelief at the simplistic joy and contentment of the people. Realisation dawns that these perceived poor tribal people are in reality truly blessed, for they unknowingly live a quality life of pure contentment, deriving pleasure from the simplest of tasks. They live for the moment, respecting all living forms, knowing that each has a specific role to play in the magnificent universal plan. These tribal groups live for the day; they have not yet learned to fret about tomorrow or the day after. As long as they have food, warmth, shelter and a sense of belonging, they are truly content. On this occasion, ignorance is truly bliss. They know no other life, have no wish to change it and would flounder and die if immersed in Western culture.

From time immemorial, humanity has questioned its existence and purpose, forever seeking the significance of ancestral civilisation. Although humanity is unique, clever and inventive, Mother Nature dictates to a certain extent our lifestyle. When this planet is bathed in rain, Mother Earth is refreshed and rejuvenated. All living matter grows. The sun emits light and warmth: the planet thrives. Take one away and the planet and everything on it shrivels and dies.

Throughout generations, humanity has tended to regard gems and metals hewn out of the ground as coveted treasure for adornment and acquisition – a measure of wealth. Our real treasure is the dawning and setting of the sun and the incredible power of wind, cloud and rainfall, without which crops would not grow. Without water and the warmth and light of the sun, we could not survive. Every living form would wither and die. Slowly, we are beginning to marvel and respect the complexities and intricacies of this majestic, beautiful planet we share – our Mother Earth.

Looking back at civilisations and dynasties of the past, we see the strength and fortitude of their intellect and knowledge. Ingenuity and wisdom was ingrained in their culture. Twenty-first century man, who has achieved so much, truly believes our legacy of success and achievement is far more advanced than those of our ancestors. Perhaps so, perhaps not! Mankind faces more and more uphill struggles in promoting world peace, and as the standard of life goes up, the quality of life goes down. We continually find ourselves questioning yet again our purpose and destiny. It calls into question why are we here on this earth plane? What is the reason for mankind? Is it purely to reproduce or is there a far greater purpose?

Many civilisations of the past believed in cycles, following the movement and realignment of the planets and constellations. They respected changing weather patterns, working with rather than against Mother Nature's varying moods. Brilliant scientists with advanced technological processes are slowly peeling back the layers of this planet's growth, researching deeply and intensively, delving back in time, trying to ascertain when and how this planet came into existence. They are investigating how Earth has evolved, asking the never-ending questions, "Why and how has the complex Earth growth ages evolved?" Do we really know and understand the dynamics of our planet? We stop and gaze in wonder at diverse and complex terrains and their eco system. Our breath is taken away at the awesome majestic beauty of nature's wonders – the Grand Canyon, Niagara Falls, glaciers, northern lights, Himalayas, volcanoes and the mystery of unchartered oceans to name but a few.

Man has always tried to pit his wits against nature. Nature allows us the grace to achieve and win occasionally, always holding back the powerful and unexpected release of untold energy which is unleashed when Mother Earth dictates. Humanity has suffered from a compulsion to achieve the impossible dream, to strive to master the seemingly impossible and unachievable – to ever elongate potential in the quest of pushing humanity to the limit, to prove an inbuilt drive that mankind can rise to the occasion and master the challenge. At the end of the day, mankind will always be at the mercy of Mother Nature.

Imagine for one visionary moment that we could fly alongside a flock of Canada geese calling while synchronising their unique V-shaped formation signalling the transition into spring, brilliantly executing the art of minimising expended energy. For one brief moment, gain an understanding of their cackling call. Visit their breeding grounds in Europe; view their wintering grounds in Canada and North America – what an experience! During the flight, we would soar high over many countries, each unique in energy, intensity and vibration. We would be strangely aware of the change of vibration as we fly over various countries, each emitting its own unique resonance, reverberating from the energy and essence of the differing nationalities.

As society changes, its people, countryside and suburbia alters, creating a huge shift in energy and vibration unknowingly felt by all living forms. A snapshot of flying with this flock of geese twenty years ago would be vastly different from one taken today. Through economic logistics, people, say, sixty years ago tended to live and work in an area where they had roots. Family ties were strong. Communities were bound together through work, friendship, struggles and joy. Their inhabitants were surrounded by familiarity, secure in a sense of belonging, where comparative safety reigned. People were on nodding terms with their closest neighbours. An unspoken support network existed – a community spirit forged.

Nowadays, peoples of the world migrate like birds to where they firmly believe lifestyle opportunities are greater, somewhere they hope they will be happy and financially better off. We now need to question, "better off" in what way? In terms of employment and social opportunities new doors of change may open, but in the long term, is a change of location any better? Are the pastures any greener? Like wildlife who travel from one location to another, seeking food and shelter, this may not always be so. What we envisage from a distance may look great until we investigate and delve deeper, sometimes being left with a sense of impatience, dissatisfaction and regret. We may find that some of the changes and desires we seek do not necessarily transform into our greatest wish. We need to acknowledge and accept that none of us lives in a perfect world.

We are but a minute speck in this wonderful universe. I believe strongly that however insignificant we may feel at times, we each have a special purpose, an important part to play in this wonderful cosmos. We hurtle through time, sometimes forgetting we are here for a reason. However, we are so busy planning for tomorrow and the following day that we forget to stop and enjoy the moment, to look and really see what is around us and surrounding us, to rejoice we are where we are at this point in time for a reason. With hindsight, relive the joy of past positive decisions, thankful for the journey trodden so far. Reflect with personal pride on the effort and tenacity expended to be where you are right now and fully appreciate how far you have travelled. Remember that time is extremely precious and not recoverable. You cannot ever relive a second of your life. You cannot buy time.

I believe humanity is undergoing a great change: our planet is struggling and rebelling at its treatment by mankind. We are now questioning our purpose, re-evaluating our lives. Our great-grandparents would be horrified at the upbeat speed of this plane and find the frenetic pace of today's society incomprehensible. They would gawp at the numerous inventions and gadgets that supposedly save time, but which we fail to use wisely. Our personal high expectations and unrealistic expectations of others are now out of kilter. Modern-day society has gained so much in advanced technological terms, but sadly in the process lost sight of how wonderful it is to breath fresh air, to see the colourful world we share, to hear laughter, birds singing, to give and feel love, belong to a family, enjoy the warmth of friendship, a community. To talk, sing, laugh and have freedom of speech. To be alive.

I believe our destiny is mapped out before we are born. We are merely a player in the vast blueprint of life and the greater cosmic plan. We are all interlinked into a vast consciousness of being, silently participating in a dramatic transformation. Leaders of past civilisations have always been in the forefront of consulting wisdom of far-seeing visionaries. There has always been a deep desire to know what is around the next corner. People's craving and appetite to know more is as strong today as it always has been.

Prophets, seers and mystics have always been consulted by the rich and famous. Faced with crucial life-changing decisions that could impact on society or alter the path of history, many historic royals and leaders of dynasties have consulted proven respected soothsayers, acting on their spoken word. Over eons of time, wise mystics have been revered, their words profound. Astrologers, shamans and the like have always had a part to play in every civilisation. Even today, some respected famous statesmen seek reassurance and guidance from those considered honourable, wise and discreet, who deliberate on predicted traits, pitfalls to avoid and give a possible glimpse into the future.

Scientists still debate and question how this can be so. Could it be these gifted people tap into a vast wealth of knowledge? Perhaps their store of wisdom and insight is attributed to many lifetimes of learning. Perhaps they are no more gifted than you or I. It may be their focus, their intent, their purpose, their trust and dedication to reveal the truth to those who genuinely seek. One of the most notable differences between humanity and the animal kingdom is that creatures instinctively know when danger looms. They know where to seek the most comfortable place to live, to hibernate in safety, travelling miles for water and the most plentiful and nourishing food. They instinctively know, listen and react to a need for survival, passed down the bloodline. Mankind has also inherited this self-same instinct for survival; we refer to it as intuition. Unfortunately, due to the frenetic pace of the twenty-first century, we do not allow ourselves either the time or space to listen and act on our intuition and the information transmitted.

With the remarkable availability of jet travel, the world appears to be shrinking. Within the space of a day or two, we can be transported across continents and oceans to the other side of the world. With barriers between countries being eroded, the world has shrunk in terms of access yet many people still appear to be lost in a wilderness of thought and focus, still seeking direction.

A time is fast approaching when the consciousness of the cosmos is changing: it will be realigned, as it has been in the past. We all need to make a positive contribution to that shift of consciousness by being true to ourselves, by listening to who we really are and having faith in guidance transmitted from the Higher Realms. To listen and respond to the still, small voice inside, no matter how crazy the guidance given seems to be. We will then be empowered to look ahead with confidence, knowing we are all part of a wonderful complete whole. Each one of us imprints an important mark on the specific significant design; the vast blueprint of creation; of a majestic great universal plan.

AWARENESS GUIDE

Awareness links to psychic (Greek word for soul) which is YOU. Your life is special. You each have a role to play. Life's journey is not a dress rehearsal, but is travelled only once, dealing out many twists and turns. Trust and listen to your higher self, your intuitive awareness. It will never let you down.

- Awareness is housed within you – YOU can link in at any time.
- Busy lives necessitate many choices and decisions. LISTEN AND TRUST – and the right answer will come to you.

- Be willing to look within. Link with the inner YOU/higher self/ instinct/soul/spiritual core/intuition.

- Learn not to question or ask "Why?" Just trust your inner voice.
- Remember that YOU have great wisdom and knowledge within your very BEING.

- The secret of inner peace and contentment is to accept yourself for who you are.
- Remember only YOU know how you truly feel.
- Only YOU know what feels right for you.
- Only YOU know your innermost thoughts privy to your hopes and dreams.
- Only YOU know the true state of your physical, emotional, intellectual and spiritual self.
- YOUR BODY is precious, needing to be in optimum health. Lavish it with care, as you would on an expensive car.
- YOU need to acknowledge and nurture your needs.
- YOU owe it to yourself to love yourself, to accept and develop your special talents and gifts.
- YOU need to remember your sensing and feeling is real to YOU, but invisible to others and will alter as circumstances change.
- Accept who YOU are. Being gentle with yourself embodies a hidden strength.

Remember the energy and sensation of:
- Being rejected, feeling let down
- Disappointment over an outcome of events
- Falling in love, the overwhelming joy
- The feeling of being loved and belonging
- The stress and relief of challenges met, the energy of striving and achieving
- Success

Trust your inner self and "JUST BE." Be the person you truly are. As you change, others will change around you and towards you, and your physical and mental health will improve. You will find serenity and inner peace. You will easily master the challenges which life besets you. Your aura will glow, reflecting your newfound trust and well-being. Consequently, everything in your world will be harmonious and perfect for YOU.

Most new ideas are condemned as being "ridiculous" until they become reality. How would the Victorians react to colour television, jet travel, the Internet, space investigation and mobile phones? In disbelief, I am sure. Herbert George Wells (1866-1946), the biologist, visionary and author, courageously explored his thoughts and imagination, writing many well-loved books. He enjoyed literary success with *The Time Machine*, engaged in frequent controversy over social and political issues with George Bernard Shaw and in 1933 wrote *Shape of Things to Come*. Who knows: in years to come it might be possible to go back and forward in time. Meanwhile we live in a complex, challenging and exciting world.

ENJOY BEING YOU

Exercise – Awareness
Note how often you listen to your intuition. Note how you feel. Note when
life patterns change.

When life patterns change.

_ _

_ _

_ _

_ _

_ _

_ _

_ _

_ _

_ _

_ _

_ _

_ _

_ _

_ _

_ _

_ _

_ _

Essence

Love, light, truth and patience
Ingredients of a special essence
Enhancing the soul, making it sweet
A radiant sight to all it meets

Love is needed along life's way
To uplift and strengthen every day
A smile with warmth, a fleeting glance
Making the heart and soul sing and dance

Truthful speaking is a painful game
Sometimes necessary just the same
To see the way things really are
Perhaps taking four steps back, looking afar

We must have enough for our needs
Surely it's beyond us all this greed
People and contentment a measure of success
Not how vast and wealthy our business

Seemingly the balance is all wrong
Lost the carefree, happy throng
"Grab all we can" now seems the motto to live
Everyone taking, no one wants to give.

Patience is a waiting game
A hard, long lesson just the same
To master the grace of all four
Must surely open heaven's door

Chapter 15
Priceless Treasure – A Reflection

Invaluable wealth and riches relating to money, precious gems, minerals or a valued person held in high esteem.

It would appear many people of all ages and cultures travel the globe in the search for the elusive fabled gold in the belief that acquiring this "prize" will transform their lives, consciously unaware that the priceless treasure they seek is closer than they realise.

Sadly, they have yet to value the awakening of spiritual guidance and upliftment, the reality yet to dawn that nothing can be accomplished by journeying to the ends of the earth in the desperate search for the elusive "cup of happiness and wealth." Little do they realise that the secret to the quarry they so earnestly seek is deep within their very being. Their consciousness is yet to be awakened to the knowledge they are spirit in a physical frame, originating from the Higher Realms, returning "home" when their time on Mother Earth is spent.

Unfortunately, today's society appears to be obsessed with image and perfection and is blind to see life played out from a wider stance. Some are seemingly unable to grasp, accept or notice that the barrage and constant bombardment of media coverage intrusively encroaches upon every aspect of our lives. Realisation evades the issue. Although in essence we have the freedom to go where we choose, in reality our movements are monitored by an increasing invasion of closed-circuit surveillance cameras. Scarier still is the creeping onslaught of cyber infiltration. Seemingly in the future, there a strong possibility our movements at work, around our home and even while enjoying our leisure activities will be monitored and scrutinised. Thankfully, our thoughts and feelings remain private, being totally invisible to others. I wonder how many of you have read George Orwell's classic book "1984" published in 1949. How scary is the realisation his fictional vision of the world is fast becoming the world we now share, his insight unfolding right before your eyes, modern man being mere key players.

Why do we fail to sense and comprehend that the lifestyle balance of modern man is distorted and totally screwy? Our seeming sense of proportion to distinguish between events we perceive as real and unreal is becoming more and more distorted. How do we measure value? What is really imperative and important in relation to our perception of importance? We need to wake up to the fact we are merely players in one enormous rolling script, hurtling into our role without stopping for an instant to ponder the mantle of the personae we chose to play. Oblivious to the realisation, we are slowly being brainwashed and programmed by others.

How saddened the celestial realms must be to witness mankind's greed and perception of want and perfection, fuelling an ever-growing consuming selfish desire. Sadly, mankind's lack of care and respect for all living forms on this extraordinary, wonderful planet is tainting and destroying a truly magical world, a world we now barely choose to see. Surely, we need to review our priorities to realise that:

We are all merely a pulsating energy in a pool of light. Encased in a core of love, encapsulating depths and levels of emotion. Many lifetimes' experiences and wisdom herald a deep need to think aright, do aright, care aright, encouraging every single soul to feel complete.

To awaken to the knowledge that God is near.

The celestial realms register our thoughts, doubts and fears, and when given permission draw close to uplift and guide. Surrender confusion, embrace clarity, an awakening – encompass joy, a priceless treasure to behold, more valuable than a rainbow's gold.

So roll away confusion and embrace clarity. From this moment on, enjoy and be thankful for each minute and second of your day. Always try to see the best in every situation; be satisfied and grateful for the life you have. Remember there is always a good and flip side to every situation. Whatever befalls you, accept and be content with the circumstance you find yourself in. Learn to go with the flow for therein lies perfect contentment and peace of mind. Master the message, "Whatever state I find myself in, therein I am content."

Be tenacious; see the best in any given situation. The modern pressure of life creates unsettlement, reinforcing the desire for perfection. When not met, it results in low self-esteem, exacerbating a low mood feeling of not keeping abreast with a perception of successful people. Joyfully accept you cannot be everything to all men. Eradicate these irrational fears. Look for the best in each day and rest assured that something or someone will inadvertently uplift you - a smile, a kind thought, word or deed.

Happiness is purely a state of mind. Holy men in India reject worldly goods, apart from clothing to protect their human form from the sun, rain and cold. They exist on a deep belief system, a euphoria of total contentment and peace. They do not doubt; they accept and know their needs will be met. Accept your conditions of life. Accept with grace and delight the simplest of pleasures. Be mindful we only see what we choose to see; others perceive us as they elect to see us. Never ever judge a book by its cover, but take time to become accustomed to the contents.

The simplest of pleasures brings the greatest joy and costs nothing. Observe the bond between a newborn baby and its mother – the instinctive emotional bond, the overwhelming joy of the miracle of life and love cannot be measured. Relive the memory of strolling by a river on a balmy summer's evening, the heady silence being broken by a chorus of birdsong prior to dusk falling, signalling a time to rest. Pure unadulterated joy does not have to contain a price tag so take time out to appreciate your achievements to date. Enjoy your hard loving input into assisting nature's creativity in the garden, hand in hand with God, creating a landscape full of colour and activity. Remember, we cannot slow down or speed up time. Everything happens at a designated time and place.

How do you define wealth or fairness? There are always those who appear to fall on their feet, people who, on the surface, appear to have everything alongside those who appear to have very little. The measure of contentment and happiness does not come from the collection of material trappings acquired; it derives from being totally content and satisfied with what one has. On reflection, it would seem that those with very little, like peoples living a simplistic life in small tribal communities, eking out an existence palatable to their needs, actually possess true wealth. Knowingly and willingly, they care and respect one another, their environment, source of nourishment and shelter, blessed in the unquestionable belief of their community. Family and surroundings create their inner peace and riches.

Irrespective of the situation you find yourself in, no matter how difficult or stressful the days may be, rejoice in being alive. Be thankful for the simple delights each day brings. Be content. Take every day as it comes and make the most of each day. Constant whinging, complaining and being discontent jars the nervous system, creating a spiral of tension and discomfort.

Remember that stillness and silence is as important as action and movement. Despite the fact we live in turbulent times, we have been given the ability to face uncertainty with a nugget of optimism once we believe and accept there is a reason for the experience we are moving through. This belief keeps us buoyant and balanced during difficult times.

Inner peace and contentment are derived from "Being," accepting and loving the essence of being you, accepting the experience of being where you are at this moment in time. Enjoy each moment, where you find yourself and what you have.

Gurus are at peace, their minds still and content. They understand and accept their purpose in this world. We could all benefit a great deal from taking their lead and gentle philosophy of life. Their lifestyle illustrates the important message of deriving pleasurable acceptance in enjoying each precious moment, movement and energy of the day. Regretfully, a vast percentage of mankind rushes eagerly through each day, waiting for tomorrow and the day after tomorrow, perpetually planning in their mind's eye for the weeks and months ahead.

Recognise negativity for what it truly is – unwanted rubbish. Question whether the accumulation is of your making or unconsciously absorbing other people's negativity. With raw honestly accept if this garbage is not discarded. It will hold you back, slowly and systematically hindering progress, destroying hopes and dreams for a fulfilling future. Allow synchronicity to awaken the immeasurable treasure chest of your true potential, unleashing hidden positive creative energies. Follow and believe in this new pointer. Focus your vision in the direction of a new circle of opportunities. Never complain or condemn. Be mindful that everyone has something to offer. We can learn from each other, so be prepared sometimes to reach beyond your feelings and learn to appreciate one another.

Believe and accept you are now balanced, centred and focussed:

- *Your spirit, mind and heart in harmony as one.*
- *You now have insight in understanding the significance of happenings in your world.*
- *You are truly content to "be," to go with the flow of life.*
- *You are blessed with inner peace, at one with yourself and all living forms.*
- *You are happy and content to be YOU.*

Irrespective of where we find ourselves in the world, we choose to celebrate our day of birth – our special day, our birthday. We view the year ahead with hope in our heart. It's another milestone. We tend to celebrate in party mood with music, food and drink flowing, more often than not choosing to share our day with close friends and family. In eager anticipation, we open cards, digesting words of love and good wishes for the year ahead. We excitedly open an array of presents lovingly chosen for us, thanking people for all the gifts, some we silently may or may not be enthralled about. For that one very special day we thrive on being the centre of attention, enjoying the wealth of generosity and warm emotion showered upon us. The delight of some presents carries us through the year, the unwanted disappointing gifts being secretly stowed away to avoid offending the giver. Our special day in the year is seemingly over in the blink of an eye.

The celestial realms who watch over us register our trials and tribulations, hopes and dreams, drawing close when asked to guide and uplift. They link with us as we celebrate another milestone reached on this earth plane. They choose to bless us with gifts of the very finest, precious gifts impossible to measure, enveloped with love and light to enhance our onward journey. These precious gifts assist mankind's earth plane journey, reinforcing optimism. An inner belief light and love reign supreme, enhancing the soul's progression.

The intent and energy of these wondrous gifts are replenished every year, the directed powerful celestial energy tempered with the passing years. These gifts are bestowed on us by the angelic realms to remind us each year of the wondrous influential Higher Realm energy encircling us on our special day. The finest gifts bestowed are the most precious mankind could ever wish for.

These priceless treasures, given with endearing love, jog a conscious memory of fulfilment and happiness as you celebrate your special day, highlighting once again the depth of care and wisdom willingly bestowed by the angelic realms. They extend an expression of unbelievable joy for you to hold close to your heart, a treasure chest of priceless gifts to sustain and uplift.

Time... to enjoy the little treasures each day holds.

Quiet... to be able to hear the stirrings of your inner heart.

Laughter... to help you overcome life's heartaches and disappointments.

Calm... to free you from problems and stress.

Friends... to bring you joy to warm your heart and make you feel at home in the world.

Dreams... to keep you going on.

The acceptance of these special gifts reignites a flame of self-belief, enabling you to cast aside the mantle created by others, obliterating pre-programmed expectations. So delight and rejoice in being YOU!

Accept and know there is within each and everyone a treasure chest brimming with priceless talents and gifts waiting to be explored. Surrender to the energy flow of your physical, emotional, intellectual and spiritual energy cycles. Find courage from time to time to declutter areas of your life and to walk away from situations and people you know hinder your progress in fulfilling your purpose.

Believe in YOU, your destiny!

There is within us all a spark of the divine.
We are in this world to build character and personality.
Whatever lies before you, have faith and climb
until you reach your dream!

Serenity

Serenity is that warm glow that
Comes alive when you know
Every sinew, bone and pore
Awakens to a lion's roar
Of hope, of dreams, a light within
Oh spirit divine, who dwells within

It encaptures every living thing
A butterfly, a bird on wing
The mighty sea, the lamb so meek
A buffalo with a stubborn streak

It reaches out to shout and sing
"Oh God, Oh God, let the angels sing"
Let the bells ring out and shout and say
"Oh thank you, God, for me and this day."